No Gluten, No Problem

No Gluten, No Problem

A Handy Guide to Celiac Disease—with Advice and 80 Recipes

Carlota Máñez

Translated by Morena Escardo

Skyhorse Publishing

The information given here is designed to help you make informed decisions about your health. It is not intended to replace the advice of a qualified health professional. If you have a condition that requires care, please seek treatment with your healthcare provider.

Original title: Vivir Sin Gluten
© 2008 Editorial Océano, S.L. (Barcelona, Spain)

Photographs: Becky Lawton

English translation © 2015 by Skyhorse Publishing

Skyhorse Publishing books may be purchased in bulk at special discounts for sales promotion, corporate gifts, fund-raising, or educational purposes. Special editions can also be created to specifications. For details, contact the Special Sales Department, Skyhorse Publishing, 307 West 36th Street, 11th Floor, New York, NY 10018 or info@skyhorsepublishing.com.

Skyhorse® and Skyhorse Publishing® are registered trademarks of Skyhorse Publishing, Inc.®, a Delaware corporation.

Visit our website at www.skyhorsepublishing.com.

10 9 8 7 6 5 4 3 2 1

Library of Congress Cataloging-in-Publication Data is available on file.

Cover design by Anna Christian
Cover photo credit Thinkstock

ISBN: 978-1-63220-326-7
Ebook ISBN: 978-1-63220-859-0

Printed in China

Contents

What is gluten?

What is gluten and why are some people sensitive to it? Before going into how a gluten-free diet can be just as tasty and healthy as a regular diet containing this protein, it's important to start at the beginning. According to the Spanish Federation of Celiac Disease (FACE), about 80 percent of processed foods sold in Spanish supermarkets contain, or could contain, gluten. These numbers show how difficult grocery shopping and cooking can be for people who are sensitive to this protein.

Gluten is a protein found in the seed of many cereals, combined with starch. It represents 80 percent of the protein in wheat, and is composed of gliadin and glutenin. Other than wheat, the cereals rye, barley, and, in many cases, oatmeal have it too. For this reason, it's smart to avoid oatmeal as well, as it can potentially contain small amounts of gluten. In its natural state, oatmeal doesn't affect people who suffer from celiac disease, but it's usually stored with wheat, so it is often contaminated with gluten, by cross-contamination. Rice, corn, sorghum, and millet, on the other hand, are completely gluten-free, which makes them safe cereals for people suffering from celiac disease.

Gluten is what gives wheat-corn its elasticity, what allows it to ferment, and what gives bread and other baked doughs that elastic and fluffy texture we all love. During the baking process, gluten traps the fermentation gases inside the dough, and that is the reason it grows. In a similar way, once the dough is cooked, gluten doesn't let the bread deflate.

You can get gluten from the flour of wheat and other cereals, by washing away the starch. You first need to form a dough by mixing the flour with water, and then keep washing it until it comes out clear. For chemical use (not food-related), it's better to mix the water with salt. After this process, you are left with a sticky and fibrous substance, similar to chewing gum. One of gluten's characteristics is that once it's cooked, it becomes firm, and absorbs the taste of the liquid it's been cooked in. This quality makes it a beloved meat substitution in vegetarian and Buddhist cuisines.

Gluten is made of a mixture of proteins, which can be classified in two groups: prolamines and glutenins. The main component in gluten is a wheat prolamin called "gliadin."

The type and amounts of prolamines in each cereal are:

Cereal	Type of Prolamin	Content percent
Wheat	Gliadin	69 percent
Rye	Secalinin	30-50 percent
Oatmeal	Avenin	16 percent
Barley	Hordein	46-52 percent
Corn	Zein	55 percent
Rice	Orzenin	5 percent
Sorghum	Kafirin	52 percent

Source: Tuotromédico.com

WATCH OUT FOR SEITAN

Seitan is an important food in most vegetarian diets, as it is a great meat substitute. However, you should keep in mind that it is made of whole wheat gluten. In fact, it is the wheat protein (gluten) that results from eliminating the germ and starch through kneading, washing, and finally cooking.

Also known as "vegetable meat," thanks to its high protein content, smell, taste, and texture, it can be used in many different ways to replace animal protein. For this reason, meat-eaters shouldn't consume too much seitan. Other than being a good source of protein, it also has high levels of vitamin B12 and iron, and it has many fewer calories than meat. Pure seitan flour (gluten) is sold in many countries.

Celiac Disease

Celiac disease is a permanent intolerance to gluten, accompanied by damage to the small intestine's lining. This reduces the gut's ability to absorb enough nutrients for the proper functioning of the sufferer's body. When foods containing gluten are consumed, the immune system of the person who suffers from this chronic intestinal problem reacts and further damages the small intestine's mucous lining. As a result, consuming this protein dangerously damages the hairlike intestinal lining, which is in charge of absorbing the nutrients from any ingested foods—minerals, vitamins, carbohydrates, proteins, and fats—and sending them to the rest of the body. When this is damaged, the body is incapable of properly assimilating nutrients, making the sufferer of celiac disease vulnerable to periods of malnutrition.

Under normal conditions, every ingested food goes through a digestive process that breaks it into smaller particles that can later be absorbed. This food absorption takes place in the small intestine, and in order for it to happen, the hairlike gut lining needs to be in place. This hairlike lining can be compared with microscopic roots that hang from the inside of the intestine. Their role in the process of nutrient absorption is similar to what the roots of a tree do, and their length is key to absorbing more or less of these nutrients. When they become shorter, absorption also decreases, and as a result, the sufferers' overall nutrition is affected.

According to the National Foundation for Celiac Awareness, celiac disease affects 1 out of every 133 Americans (1 percent). This disease can occur at any stage of life. Both in children and adults, when the symptoms are clear, it's easy to discover the cause, which can be confirmed with an intestinal biopsy. The problem is that sometimes there are no symptoms, or these are very mild, which delays the diagnosis, possibly creating many health problems in the meantime.

Allergy vs. Intolerance

The term "food allergy" is often confused with the term "food intolerance." According to the European Council of Food Information (EUCIF), food intolerances can have symptoms that are similar to those of a food allergy (amongst them, nausea, diarrhea, and stomach pain); however, the immune system does not play a role in those reactions. Food intolerances take place when the body can't properly digest a type of food, or one of its components. People with real food allergies generally need to eliminate the aggravating food completely from their diets, but people who suffer from a food intolerance can consume small quantities of the food or component they are sensitive to, without getting any symptoms (except in the case of gluten or sulphite).

The two most common food intolerances are to dairy and gluten. The latter, as we have already pointed out, is an intestinal disorder that happens when the body is sensitive to it. If the patient consumes something that contains gluten, the lining of the small intestine is damaged, and its capacity to absorb essential nutrients such as fats, proteins, carbohydrates, minerals, and vitamins decreases. Amongst its symptoms, the most usual ones are diarrhea, weight loss, fatigue, moodiness, and abdominal pain. In children, symptoms caused by malnutrition, such as growth problems, may appear. At the moment, the only way to help patients suffering from celiac disease is by putting them on a completely gluten-free diet. A list of gluten-free foods can usually be found in diet information centers, and in centers of support related to celiac disease. When gluten is removed from the diet, the intestine gradually regenerates, and symptoms start to disappear.

Current research is trying to identify the nature and exact consequences of the amino acids found in gluten that produce celiac disease, and this information may have a great impact on the use of biotechnology and the development of cereal crops that will not cause any kind of sensitivity in the future.

Causes

When gluten comes in contact with the inner lining of the small intestine, a reaction that pushes the immune system to mistakenly attack it like an external aggressor is produced. What causes this exactly is still unknown, but there is certainly a strong genetic component in all of this.

Is it hereditary? Celiac disease cannot be qualified as a congenital disease. This means that nobody is born with this disease. However, there is a genetic predisposition to suffer from it, passed from parents to kids, which doesn't necessarily mean that the child will develop it throughout his or her life. Thirty percent of people have these sensitive genes, but not all of them develop the disease.

If the father, mother, or siblings suffer from celiac disease, the chance of the child also suffering from it is 10 percent. If you have an identical twin with celiac disease, your chances of getting it raise to over 70 percent. Therefore, when a family member is diagnosed with celiac disease, it's very important that the rest of the family gets tested too.

Symptoms can appear for the first time right after birth, but this ailment can remain dormant until a particular situation triggers it to manifest: a surgery, pregnancy, viral infection, or period of emotional stress, for example.

One of the most thorough studies ever done about celiac disease in identical and non-identical twins was done by a group of researchers at the University of Naples, in 2002.

By comparing genetically similar identical twins, and non-identical twins who only share the same number of genes, like most siblings do, the researchers were able to show to what extent an ailment is genetic, and to what extent it's influenced by a shared environment.

The study found that environmental factors have little to no effect on digestive ailments that cause diarrhea, weight loss, abdominal distention, and damage in the small intestine. The scientists determined that there are many genes acting together when the disease takes place.

The results were based on blood samples from 47 pairs of identical and non-identical twins, where at least one of the twins had been diagnosed with celiac disease. The results published in *Gut* magazine pointed out that in 38 percent of the pairs, both the twins had signs of celiac disease (75 percent of the identical twins, and 11 percent of the non-identical twins). It was also found that women who had a twin were 35 percent more likely to suffer from celiac disease than a male twin.

AN ANCIENT DISEASE

In the second century BC, Areteus of Cappadocia already described "the celiac affliction" and its treatment, commenting that diet was the most important part of the treatment, and that floury foods had to be kept to the minimum. He added that if the patient was able to cure him/herself, this would be thanks to the effects of a change in the diet.

Despite this, many centuries passed until Samuel Gee gave the first modern description of this disease at a conference at the Children's Hospital of Great Ormond Street in London, in 1887. His fascination for medical history, and his ability to read ancient Greek, allowed Gee to become well acquainted with the work of Areteus of Cappadocia about celiac disease. In his report, Gee wrote: "There is a kind of chronic indigestion in people of all ages, but particularly in children from 1 to 5 years old. It is manifested through the feces, which are watery, pale, and smelly…"

Many years later, in 1950, two Dutch researchers called Dike and Van Kamer finally found the clear relation between gluten consumption and the development of this disease. Both researchers had noticed that during the war famine, when people couldn't eat bread, those suffering from celiac disease got better. This observation led to several studies that concluded in the discovery of the food causing this ailment.

In the '60s, celiac disease began to be diagnosed and treated in Europe, and then around the world with a diet of bananas and acidifying milk. Not much later, in 1968, the first celiac disease association was founded in England.

What are the symptoms?

Celiac disease usually develops between the second and third year of life for children with a predisposition to it, who started consuming gluten around the seventh or eighth month of life. The first contact with gluten usually comes in the form of baby porridges, bread, cookies, or through other foods that have it.

Gluten-related diarrhea is usually bulky and pale (not necessarily too frequent), and tends to be accompanied by vomit, distention of the belly, general discomfort, weight loss, and mood change (bad temper or shyness). In its worst form (celiac crisis), there's dehydration, skin bruises, digestive hemorrhage, and fluid retention. However, the problem can begin earlier in life, or, on the other hand, at an adult age. In any case, there is a period free of symptoms between the time a person starts consuming gluten, and the time when the disease develops.

The symptoms for this condition are varied, and they can change at different stages in life:

- Before presenting symptoms, children usually have a good state of health and nutrition. If they have been consuming flours containing gluten, they will start having diarrhea, smelly and bulky feces with a grayish color, vomit, significant loss of appetite and weight loss, fatigue, and abdominal bloating, before they turn three. After the age of three, soft stools remain a constant, growing is slow, they suffer from anemia that is resistant to treatment, and changes in the personality begin to happen. What develops is a state of being known as "celiac habit": sad appearance, indifference, and apathy. Performance in school can diminish. Muscles can be weak, and there may be some paleness, a dry tongue, mouth sores, a bloated belly, and flat buttocks.

- During adolescence, the disease usually doesn't cause these symptoms. In fact, at this time of life it tends to be asymptomatic, which can be dangerous because it makes the diagnosis more difficult. For this reason, it's important that when faced with chronic or intermittent diarrhea accompanied by weight loss and a decrease in appetite, anemia (without having lost significant amounts of blood), hypocalcemia, and vitamin and mineral deficiencies during the teenage or adult years of someone's life, celiac disease is suspected. When a patient doesn't receive treatment, the loss of teeth enamel is also common.

When should a baby start consuming gluten? It's recommended that gluten isn't introduced in a baby's diet until he or she is six months old. A study was published in the *JAMA* journal in 2005, where 1,560 babies were observed for five years to find out if the time when gluten is introduced to the diet is a factor in developing the disease. The study found that children who started eating gluten before their fourth month were five times more susceptible to developing celiac disease than those who started eating it when they were between four and six months old. Children who didn't try gluten until after their seventh month had a slightly higher risk. The results suggest that children who are prone to develop celiac disease should start consuming gluten when they are around six months old, since waiting longer doesn't seem to lower the risk. These findings don't differ from the general recommendations as to when to start introducing gluten in a baby's diet.

Symptoms of celiac disease

There is a large variability in the symptoms, and these are not always related to the digestive system. The symptoms presented by patients suffering from celiac disease depend on the deficiency of nutrient absorption from the diet. According to the Celiac Association of Madrid, these days it's more common to present symptoms outside of the intestines, and just a few intestinal symptoms that may be very mild and hard to catch. To be more precise, around 50 percent of the new diagnosed cases in children, and 65 percent of adults, don't show intestinal symptoms.

Gastrointestinal Symptoms:

- Abdominal pain.
- Chronic or occasional diarrhea.
- Lactose intolerance (common at the time of diagnosis, and generally solved with the treatment).
- Floating, bloody, bad smelling, and greasy stools.
- Nausea and vomit.
- Inexplicable weight loss (although people may also be overweight at the time of being diagnosed).
- Diminished appetite (it can also increase or remain the same).
- Abdominal distention, bloating, gas, indigestion.
- Constipation.

Others:

- Anemia: it's one of the most common extra-intestinal manifestations, and the most common initial clinical manifestation.
- Pain in the bones and joints.
- Bone disease (osteoporosis, fracture, kyphoscoliosis)
- Insufficient breathing caused by anemia.
- Easy bruising.
- Defects and de-coloration in the tooth enamel.
- Retarded growth in children.
- Hair loss.
- Hypoglycemia (low blood sugar levels).
- Malnutrition.
- Mouth ulcers.
- Nose bleeding.
- Convulsions.
- Unusually short height.
- Skin disorders (dermatitis).
- General or abdominal bloating.
- Deficiencies of mineral, vitamins, and essential nutrients (like iron, folate, vitamin K).
- Depression.
- Fatigue.

■ Irritability and change in behavior.
■ Muscle cramps.

Some people with celiac disease don't present any symptoms, because the damaged part of their intestine is capable of absorbing enough nutrients to prevent them. However, even people without symptoms are at risk of suffering from the complications associated with this disease.

How is it diagnosed?

The disease is frequently diagnosed at infancy, by the end of the breastfeeding period—which is when cereals are first introduced in the diet—although it can be diagnosed at any age. Symptoms can be subtle although the patient may not feel completely well at times, for no apparent reason, until being diagnosed. When the condition presents symptoms that are mostly outside of the intestines, and which are very mild, it's difficult to get a quick diagnosis, and a gluten-free diet is not implemented for a long time. In adults, it usually takes up to ten years between the beginning of the symptoms and getting properly diagnosed, with the related increase in cancer risk and other severe pathologies.

Another fact: according to the National Foundation for Celiac Awareness, 83 percent of Americans with the disease are undiagnosed or misdiagnosed. Many people have not been diagnosed and suffer symptoms such as diarrhea, vomiting, hair loss, iron deficiency, and enamel problems, amongst others.

Celiac disease is one of the hardest conditions to detect, especially in adults, because the symptoms are very similar to those caused by other afflictions, and range from loss of appetite to gastroenteritis. For this reason, other than having been diagnosed based on the symptoms, it's important to get blood work and an intestinal biopsy done.

When the patient fills out a health history, the doctor will ask about any symptoms, as well as the frequency of elimination and the appearance, consistency, and color of the stools. He will also want to know if there has been any weight loss, or if there seems to be anemia (fatigue, pale skin). In most cases, he will explore the abdomen, and check for blisters in the skin or ulcers in the mouth.

After studying the physical examination, initial studies usually consist in blood work. The doctor will try to detect any iron, folic acid, or calcium deficiency, amongst other readings. But there's another type of blood analysis that focuses on detecting antibodies (which are part of the immune system) that are frequently found, although not always, in the presence of celiac disease. The most common antibody found when there is celiac disease is called anti-endomisium, and it targets an enzyme called "tissue transglutaminase." Other antibodies found are anti-gliadin, anti-reticulin, and anti-transglutaminase. If these are detected in the blood, the probabilities of celiac disease being present are high.

From this point on, an effective way to confirm the existence of this disease is to study a biopsy from the small intestine lining, generally obtained through a gastroscopy. Some countries have screening campaigns for celiac disease, to determine the levels of antibodies reacting to gluten in members of the general population who don't present symptoms. In every case, due to the hereditary component of this disease, a study of the direct relatives (children, siblings, parents) of anyone suffering from celiac disease is advised. The results come out positive in 10 percent of the cases. The more this diagnosis and the following treatment is delayed, the higher the probabilities of suffering from malnutrition and other complications.

Even though tests and analysis can point in a certain direction, the only completely reliable source to establish the presence of celiac disease with certainty is an intestinal biopsy before removing gluten from the diet, and after reintroducing it once the injury is healed.

The biopsy is not dangerous as long as it is carried out by an experienced practitioner. A catheter goes through the esophagus and the stomach, all the way to the top part of the small intestine, where a small sample of intestinal lining is taken to be analyzed under a microscope. In cases of celiac disease, it is typical to find some damage in this lining due to the toxic effect of gluten. This test can be done at any age as long as the presence of celiac disease is suspected. No anesthesia or admission to the hospital is required (the patient only needs to remain on the premises for a few hours to be under observation). The procedure is not painful, but it may be uncomfortable as the patient needs to swallow a capsule connected to the catheter (similar to a small cable), which can cause nausea.

The first intestinal biopsy takes place when there is suspicion of celiac disease, and before getting off gluten. The procedure tends to confirm the diagnosis. It is usually recommended to do it again after several months without gluten in the diet, to make sure the gut lining is healing. Once the disease is diagnosed, regular checkups are very important for a patient with celiac disease, because an increasing number of pathologies are starting to be related to this pathology, such as autoimmune diseases, thyroid disease, and problems in the pancreas.

It's been recently proven that an early diagnosis, and the resulting removal of gluten from the diet, can protect the patient from these complications related to the disease. These complications don't distinguish between patients with symptoms and patients without symptoms. Anyone who feels protected because they haven't lost 30 pounds or has never had diarrhea is wrong: only a gluten-free diet can protect him.

Future Diagnostics. An intestinal biopsy is the best and most reliable method to determine if a person suffers from celiac disease. However, the days of this test may be counted. The European Project CD-MEDICS, led by researchers from the University Rovira y Virgili (Spain), would allow doctors to detect celiac disease with just one drop of blood and a biosensor. This chip would analyze the blood and detect the antibodies developed by patients who have celiac disease when they ingest the proteins of gluten, which are toxic to them. On top of this, the test will determine how everybody would react when eating gluten. This new method would eliminate the uncomfortable intestinal biopsies that are used today.

What is gluten provocation? Another way to diagnose celiac disease, but not very common, is provocation with gluten. In this process, gluten is reintroduced in the diet to confirm the disease. It's important to do this under the guidance of a physician, and when a biopsy hasn't been specific enough. Although the provocation phase of a gluten lesion is important to get a definite diagnosis in some cases, it's advisable to wait until the patient is at least six years old, to avoid inducing lesions in the teeth enamel, which would be irreversible. It's not recommended to do this type of testing during adolescence, so as not to stop the normal development of puberty. This gluten provocation shouldn't be attempted in those who suspect that they have celiac disease, and who suffer from another autoimmune disease, or any other severe chronic illness.

In most patients with celiac disease, damage in the intestinal villi appears during the first few months of introducing gluten in the diet, during the provocation stage. However, experience has also demonstrated that a small number of patients don't experience any symptoms after the gluten provocation period, and even their clinical biopsies come out normal. In these cases, after being monitored for eight years or longer, it's possible to see a relapse of damage in the gut lining, which is healed once gluten is taken out of the diet permanently. There is no good explanation for this delayed symptomatology, although in some cases it's related to a very limited ingestion of gluten.

Conditions related to celiac disease

- **Skin celiac disease.** Dermatitis herpetiformis is a skin affliction that causes a chronic eruption of blisters, warts, and lesions similar to urticaria. This skin condition is also known as skin celiac disease, as it is related in many cases to a damaged gut lining, which responds well to gluten elimination. The treatment is thus the same as the one given for celiac disease.

  To diagnose dermatitis herpetiformis, a health history and a medical exam is needed, as well as a skin biopsy with immunofluorescence (a specific type of dye that helps detect the presence of IgA antibodies). In 90 percent of the cases, intestinal damage caused by celiac disease is also present; however, that tends to be less severe, and be less extended. In any case, whether a person shows intestinal damage or not, the treatment for dermatitis herpetiformis is having a gluten-free diet. Healing the skin generally takes longer than healing the intestinal lining, but diet is essential. Many studies have proven that there is an intestinal alteration that is found in all patients, but only to a very variable degree. Similarly, approximately

20 percent of people with celiac disease are prone to develop dermatitis herpetiformis.

■ **Celiac disease and diabetes.** Sometimes the immune system reacts against us; this is what happens in the case of celiac disease and diabetes. The link is so strong that it's now advisable to test diabetic patients for celiac disease and to consider them an at-risk group. The symptoms you should watch for include: an exaggerated appetite, intense thirst, abundant urine, or inexplicable weight loss. It is estimated that about 5-6 percent of people with type 1 diabetes mellitus develop celiac disease, but only 0.4 percent of people with celiac disease develop diabetes.

■ **Others.** On top of dermatitis herpetiformis and type 1 diabetes mellitus (or insulin-dependent), there are other disorders that are related to celiac disease:
  — *Down Syndrome:* more than 15 percent of people with celiac disease have this syndrome.
  — *Thyroid disease:* People with celiac disease are more likely to develop an autoimmune thyroid condition (four times more likely to develop hypothyroidism and three times more likely to develop hyperthyroidism).
  — *Liver disease:* This condition appears in those people suffering from celiac disease who haven't received treatment. The milder cases can be reverted when gluten is eliminated from the diet.

Complications if left untreated

A gluten-free diet needs to be followed carefully and continually. The reason for this is that when this disease is not treated properly, it can cause complications that can be potentially mortal. Untreated celiac disease will manifest itself with a complication of symptoms, which can include problems that are not usually considered to be related to celiac disease, but that depend on it. Even a late diagnosis or breaking of the diet puts the patient at risk of developing related conditions such as infertility, spontaneous miscarriages, osteoporosis, fractures, some kinds of intestinal cancers, and other autoimmune diseases.

It's true—people with celiac disease can suffer from bone and muscle disorders, such as osteoporosis, osteomalacia, and tetany. These disorders are caused by a deficiency in calcium and vitamin D, due to the inefficient nutrient absorption or assimilation.

According to the Celiac Association of Madrid, there is also a much higher incidence of neurologic disorders in patients with celiac disease, which are already evident in childhood, and even more so in adulthood. Such disorders include headaches, hypotonia, learning and behavioral disabilities, delays in the psychomotor development, epilepsy, ataxia, and sensory peripheral neuropathy. Some of these disorders, such as hypotonia, can be solved after a few years with the appropriate gluten-free diet.

Epilepsy is also ten times more frequent amongst people who suffer from celiac disease. Some epilepsies are known to be caused by calcifications in the occipital lobule of the brain of patients with celiac disease, and in these cases it's possible that medication doesn't work. If untreated, celiac disease can generate anemia, bone alterations, and, in strange cases, some types of cancer. There are studies showing that following a gluten-free diet for five or more years reduces the patient's risk of suffering from all the cancers related to this condition, compared to the general population's average.

During childhood, growth may be delayed, whereas during adolescence, the first menstruation can also be delayed.

The most important aspect of the treatment is eliminating any product containing gluten from the diet. This is usually enough to see an improvement, or even a complete recovery of the gut's lining. However, lesions will reappear if gluten is reintroduced to the diet.

In most cases, a gluten-free diet results in the normalizing of the epithelial lining of the intestine. Thus, the disease can be "cured," but only if foods containing gluten are avoided. If you suffer from it, keep in mind that you can have a good quality of life in the long run, free of symptoms and complications.

In women. Some women with celiac disease have difficulty getting pregnant, and this could actually be the clue that leads them to the diagnosis. Recurring spontaneous miscarriages also happen in relation to celiac disease sometimes. Some women are also diagnosed during pregnancy, because their intestines cannot absorb sufficient amounts of iron and vitamins to satisfy the increased demands caused by pregnancy, so they develop serious anemia. Similarly, women with celiac disease tend to have underweight babies (due to intrauterine development delays caused by a nutrient deficiency). This also happens if the father is the one who suffers from celiac disease. This condition is also related to male and female infertility, menstrual cycle problems, delayed menstruation, and early menopause (from two to four years), in patients with celiac disease, with an increased risk of osteoporosis. These problems can be reverted to a big extent once a gluten-free diet is adopted.

What is the treatment?

Even though celiac disease can't be prevented, adopting a gluten-free diet can revert the lesions in the small intestine. This requires great discipline.

As a matter of fact, the only treatment for celiac disease consists of staying away from any foods containing gluten for life, even for those who have it in minimal amounts. Keep in mind, however, that gluten should never be eliminated without undergoing a stomach biopsy first to justify it.

Once a gluten-free diet is adopted, recovery may not be instantaneous, and it may take up to two years for new biopsies to come out normal. This diet does help to improve the symptoms within two weeks from starting it, blood work comes out normal within six to twelve months, and the lining of the intestine takes around two years to heal from the beginning of the treatment.

When the disease first manifests, some people may experience a temporary lactose intolerance, and sometimes also a temporary intolerance to fat. In this initial stage, a lactose and fat intolerance test should be done. When the symptoms have been controlled, milk and dairy products should progressively be added to the diet, and fat consumption can also increase, taking each person's tolerance into consideration.

This diet must be followed strictly and indefinitely, as it's been proven that even small quantities of gluten can severely damage the villi.

Many foods contain gluten, and this protein is also present in many additives used in processed foods—hence the complication of eating a completely gluten-free diet. Since this diet must be maintained for a lifetime, it's always advisable to learn which foods and which brands are safe, so the quality of life is not affected by so many dietary restrictions.

The main pillar of the treatment is the rigorous exclusion of gluten from the diet, so it's of the utmost importance to know which foods can or cannot be consumed, and to purchase only ready-made products that state that they are "gluten-free" or something similar on the label (later we will discuss how this doesn't always guarantee that a product is free from gluten).

Doctors warn about the importance of reading labels carefully when it comes to medications as well, to figure out if one of the components is gluten, and this should always be kept in mind when a patient needs to take medication. The pharmacist and doctor should always be informed of this.

In severe cases, the doctor can prescribe fat-soluble vitamins, or other immediate nutrients.

WHERE IS GLUTEN HIDDEN?

Gluten is found in breads, muffins, pastries, sweets, pasta, cereals, and also in some prepared soups, sauces, and dressings. There is also "hidden" gluten in some foods such as breakfast cereals, diet bars, potato chips, and other products offered as snacks in bars or restaurants. Certain cooking oils, particularly the ones that contain a mix of vegetable oils, can contain wheat germ oil, so it is advisable to stick to olive oil or sunflower oil. Soy sauce, mustard, and commercial mayonnaise contain gluten. Beer, whisky, and bourbon are made with cereals containing gluten, although other alcoholic beverages, such as wine and cider, are free of this substance. Of course, and as we will see in the next few pages, there are also many products that are completely gluten-free, such as all fruits, vegetables, rice, corn, nuts, potatoes, red meats, chicken and other birds, fish, eggs, and dairy, which should become the base of a gluten-free diet.

BETTER NOURISHED?

Since gluten is not a necessary protein, if the diet is varied enough and balanced, gluten can easily be replaced by other animal and vegetarian proteins that are found in many foods, such as meats, fish, eggs, milk, cheese, legumes, fruits and vegetables of any kind, and gluten-free cereals such as corn or rice. This is not all; it has even been proven that a person with celiac disease who follows the right diet eats better and in a much healthier and more balanced way than the average person. This is also the case for teenagers, because at that age people are prone to suffer from nutritional deficiencies whether they test positive for celiac disease or not, due to an unhealthy diet and a diet low in calories.

FIGHTING CONSTIPATION

When gluten is removed from the diet, some products containing gluten that also contain a lot of fiber (bread, cookies, pastries, breakfast cereals, wheat germ, etc.) are also avoided. This is the reason why a gluten-free diet tends to be low in fiber and frequently causes an alteration in the intestinal rhythm, with a tendency toward constipation. Here are some recommendations to avoid this:

— Eat 2 to 3 portions of vegetables that are rich in fiber (one portion is approximately 7 ounces, or 200 grams, of the cooked product) every day. These include peas, spinach, chard, green beans, raw tomatoes, etc.

— Eat 2 to 3 portions of raw fruits per day, if possible with the skin on.

— Eat legumes 4 times a week.

— Eat whole grain products whenever this is possible (brown rice, gluten-free whole grain cookies, etc.).

— Drink plenty of liquid, particularly water and natural juices (at least 6 cups a day).

— Eat slowly and chew the food well. Eat at the same time every day.

— Get in the habit of going to the bathroom at the same time every day, making sure you give yourself enough time to go and are not rushed.

— Practice moderate exercise every day.

— Avoid taking laxatives, as they can produce the so-called lazy gut effect, which is the result of your body's getting used to taking medication to be able to properly defecate.
— If the constipation persists, try taking flax seeds, rice germs, or plants such as fleawort (*Plantago Psyllium*).

How fleawort helps. Its mucilage richness explains the mild laxative effect, which doesn't irritate the intestinal walls. That is why it's prescribed when there is celiac disease, and also in other digestive disorders such as heartburn, irritable bowel syndrome, ulcerative colitis, and urinary problems such as cystitis.

To macerate it: Add one tablespoon of seeds to some water, and leave it soaking for half an hour. This must be drunk on an empty stomach with another glass of water, first thing in the morning. It's better, however, to take the ready-made version either in capsule form or powder, and to remember to drink plenty of water to get its beneficial effects. If there is any abdominal pain beforehand, it shouldn't be taken without consulting with a doctor first.

Diet recommendations

The main and only treatment for celiac disease is a gluten-free diet. To better learn what can be consumed and what is forbidden in this diet, and most importantly, why, we will start this chapter talking about the group of foods that contains the highest levels of this protein.

Cereals and gluten

As we've mentioned from the beginning of this book, gluten is a protein found mainly in wheat, but also in other cereals like barley, rye, and oatmeal. That is why it's important to understand which cereals can be safely consumed by people with celiac disease, and which should be avoided. It's a good opportunity to mention their nutritional benefits as well.

Those containing gluten

- **Wheat.** This is the best known cereal for having a high content of gluten.

It is also the most grown around the world, and it is the main ingredient in the diet of many civilizations. This cereal has many positive nutrients (carbohydrates, proteins, fiber, selenium, magnesium, manganese, copper, and B vitamins), but it also contains high amounts of gluten. Since wheat is consumed in many different ways, people who are intolerant to that protein should be careful with these:

— **Flour:** obtained by grinding the grains in a stone or steel mill. This process separates the germ, making the flour easier to digest, but lower in fiber.

— **Couscous:** wheat flour paste shaped like semolina, which is the base of many famous dishes such as tabbouleh.

— **Bulgur:** this is durum wheat that has been slightly sprouted, presteamed, dried in the sun, crushed, and sifted. This procedure turns it into a product that is very easy to store, and that is cooked quickly and is easy to digest.

— **Pasta:** in all its different forms, it is made with durum wheat semolina.

— **Seitan:** made with wheat germ, it's rich in trace elements, vitamin B and E, and especially in protein, giving it the name of "vegetarian meat."

— **Wheat germ:** this is a complete food in and of itself, as it contains the highest concentration of proteins, fatty acids, and vitamins. It's used in flakes to be added to yogurt, juice, etc., and also as a dietary supplement.

■ **Barley.** This cereal has many nutritious qualities, including a high content of vitamin B3 or niacin (good for the skin, the nervous system, and to avoid menstrual cramps), vitamin E (one of the anti-aging vitamins), potassium, phosphorus, and magnesium. It re-mineralizes and is a mild laxative (ideal during pregnancy), and also beneficial for the respiratory system.

It is consumed in flour (mixed with wheat, which is the base of the famous dark German bread), as a soluble powder that can be added to milk, in malt (a good coffee substitute made of fermented, sprouted, and toasted barley, which is very easy to digest, even for kids), in flakes (used in soups, or with milk as a breakfast or snack), and in whole grain form. The latter needs to cook for 60 to 70 minutes in twice its amount in water, having been previously soaked for several hours. It can be served mixed with steamed vegetables.

Rye. This is the cereal used to make the bread consumed in Northern Europe. Its flour gives the dough a granulated texture, and its characteristic, slightly bitter taste. Breads, cookies, and croquettes can be made with it. Rye bread is really made with a mixture of rye and wheat flour so it acquires the right volume and fluffiness, as this cereal has much less gluten than wheat. The higher the percentage of gluten in bread, the flatter and denser it is. The result of this flour mixture is a compact bread with an intense flavor, and that can be stored for longer periods. It is known that cultures that consume it regularly suffer from less cardiovascular disease, thanks to its blood thinning properties, and because it makes the veins and arteries more flexible. This is the result of its flavonoid content, and it is recommended to people with high blood pressure.

This bread is very rich in fiber, iron, copper, zinc, magnesium, potassium, B vitamins (B1, B2, B6, and B8), and vitamin E. Its high mucilage content also gives it slight laxative properties.

Another way of consuming it is a cooked whole grain. However, even though they're very nutritious, the grains are very hard and not recommended for weak digestive systems.

Its flakes can also be used in different preparations such as muesli.

■ **Oatmeal.** This is one of the most complete cereals. Thanks to its energetic and nutritious qualities, it has been the nutritional base of many people and civilizations, such as the Scottish, Irish, and some people in the Asian mountains.

Oatmeal is full of rich proteins, carbohydrates, fats, and a great number of vitamins, minerals, and trace elements. It also contains six out of eight essential amino acids needed for proper protein synthesis in the body. Thus, combining oatmeal with different types of whole foods makes its amino acid proportion even better, making it almost ideal for the body.

Oatmeal is also the cereal with the highest percentage of fat from a non-animal source. Sixty-five percent of its fats are unsaturated fatty acids, and 35 percent are linoleic acid. One cup (100 grams) of oatmeal flakes covers a third of our daily needs of essential fatty acids. On the other hand, oatmeal is also high in carbohydrates of slow absorption and easy assimilation. They provide energy for an extended period after being absorbed by the digestive system, and don't cause the typical fatigue or weakness the body experiences when the body's glucose goes down again (hypoglycemia).

On top of all these essential components, oatmeal has other elements that are not as important from a nutritional standpoint, but are needed for the proper functioning of the gut. We are talking about insoluble substances that are ingested with food, and which aren't absorbed by the intestine. They are extremely important for good digestion. We are talking about "fiber." This important part of the food increases the volume in the digestive tract, helping prevent and eliminate constipation.

Another recognized characteristic of oatmeal is its value as a source of energy and vitality. This makes it ideal for those who want to have more energy: students and people without strength, who feel sleepy, down, or stressed all the time.

Nevertheless, people who are intolerant to gluten should stay away from oatmeal, as it can contain small amounts of gluten. On its own, oatmeal doesn't usually make the symptoms of a person with celiac disease worse, but it's very commonly stored in the same barns as gluten, making it susceptible to being contaminated with gluten.

Those not containing gluten. Gluten is predominantly found in cereals such as wheat, rye, barley, and oatmeal. There are, however, other cereals that don't contain it and that can be eaten without a problem. They are also highly nutritive and versatile in the kitchen, making them easy to enjoy in many different ways.

- **Quinoa.** Its botanical name is *Chenopodium quinoa Willd*, and it's been grown in the South American Andes region since ancestral times. Ancient Incas called it "the mother grain" and venerated it as a sacred plant. It grows in completely organic conditions, and this keeps it free from chemical substances such as pesticides, chemical fertilizers, etc. Specific climate conditions are needed to grow it; specifically an altitude 9850 feet (3000 meters) above sea level, which explains why it was used by the indigenous people of this area as a staple in their diet instead of rice, which doesn't grow well in those conditions. Even today, the quinoa found in health food stores comes from traditional Peruvian crops, which are free from chemical products.

Quinoa is actually not a cereal, but a vegetable, but it is considered to be similar to wheat, corn, rice, and other cereals due to its composition and the way it is used. Quinoa stands out for its high protein content (14-16 percent of its weight), with such a balanced proportion of amino acids that they are as effective in the body as meat. This is why it's considered an excellent complement to strict vegetarian diets. It also provides large quantities of vitamins C, E, and B. It is highly digestive, and can be sprouted to multiply its nutrients. It also provides calcium and iron.

Quinoa can be easily stored for long periods of time without the threat of parasites or insects. It is slowly cooked for 12 minutes, with twice the amount of water.

This ingredient is free of gluten, and its flour can be used to make breads, pastries, and cookies, as we will show later on. It can be used instead of couscous or rice, as it has a very neutral taste, and a texture that combines perfectly well with both sweet and savory ingredients. Once it's cooked, it can be used as a side dish to a varied range of dishes, in particular to salads or any kind of vegetables.

- **Buckwheat.** Buckwheat (*Polygonum fagopyrum*) is originally from Central Asia: some authors claim it came from China, and others from Siberia. Just like quinoa and amaranth, buckwheat is not a cereal in classic botanical terms, but a seed from the polygonaceae family. Nutritionally, it can be considered a classic cereal thanks to its composition. Starch is its main carbohydrate; its energetic power is due to the presence of complex carbohydrates (manose, galactose, xylose and glucuronic acid). That is where its capacity to liberate so much energy comes from.

  Another of its virtues is its high proteic index, as it is rich in certain amino acids that are lacking in conventional cereals. One of them is lysine. Being completely free from gluten makes it an appropriate food for people with celiac disease.

This cereal is very well balanced, containing high doses of essential fatty acids, and 10 percent proteins. Its magnesium content makes it ideal for people in a weakened physical and mental state. Buckwheat is the only cereal containing vitamin P, a flavonoid usually found in the peel of citrus fruits that strengthens the blood vessels and prevents strokes, bleeding, hypertension, cardiovascular problems, and damage caused by radiation. Buckwheat also has vitamins B1, B2, and B3, in twice the amount as brown rice. It also contains vitamin E (tocopherol), phospholipids (choline), and linoleic acid (omega 6). This essential fatty acid represents a third of its fat content. These elements benefit the circulatory system. Unlike other cereals, buckwheat's germ is contained in the center of the grain, so peeling it doesn't lower its vital components.

Buckwheat is very rich in magnesium and potassium, with a higher iron and phosphorus content than conventional cereals. It's also high in calcium, sodium, sulfur, chlorine, iodine, and manganese. It provides high levels of fiber, which is very useful to regulate the digestive system.

Buckwheat flour is the main ingredient of the famous Brittany crepes, and when toasted, it is known as "kasha," a typical Eastern European dish. This food is consumed as a flour (it's the best to make crepes, battered foods, and desserts), in flakes, and whole.

Kasha is very popular amongst kids thanks to its mild flavor. To make it, cook it with one and a half times its volume in water, for 15-20 minutes. You can then add vegetables, chicken, meat, or others.

■ **Rice.** This is the main food of two thirds of the world's population. It's the base ingredient of 17 countries in Asia and the
Pacific, 8 countries in Africa, 7 countries in Latin America
and the Caribbean, and one of the Near East.

This is a healthy and nutritious cereal, and has qualities that
make it ideal for any kind of diet or nutritional requirement.
Starch is its main component, making it a good source of
energy. Half a cup of brown rice (100 grams) has 350 calories, 7 percent proteins and B vitamins. It's poor in minerals,
especially iron, calcium, and zinc, so it's always advisable to
combine it with legumes, vegetables, meats, or fish.

Its low fat content makes it a great food to maintain good
cardiovascular health, as long as it is cooked without
added fat.

In many culinary traditions, rice is milled, resulting in unpol-
ished rice. This process reduces the cooking time, but makes
it less shelf-stable, and eliminates a high amount of nutrients,
amongst them proteins, fiber, fat, iron, and B vitamins. This is
why consuming brown rice is recommended. In some countries, the rice grains are parboiled to lock their nutrients in
the grain. Sometimes they are fortified with added vitamins
and essential minerals too. Unfortunately, this practice has
not been adapted in many of the countries that consume rice,
as they don't have the right infrastructure for this procedure.

Types of rice

— *Long and thin rice*: it's very dry and the grains are loose once
cooked, making it ideal for salads.
— *Glutinous rice*: it has a high starch content; the grains become
sticky when cooked. The grain is short, and ideal for Italian
recipes like risotto made with Arborio or Carnaroli rice. Other
kinds of short rice grains are used for Asian dishes, such as sushi.

— *Wild rice*: this is a water plant, not a real rice, and it is grown in Canada and the United States. It's thinner than long grain rice, and has a dark color. When cooked it remains whole, and it's used for decoration more than for its particular culinary qualities.

— *Parboiled rice*: it has the same nutritional value as brown rice, and its same golden color, although it becomes white when cooked. Thanks to the special procedure of parboiling it, it doesn't overcook or become sticky, although it does take longer to cook and absorbs fewer flavors from the other ingredients it is cooked with.

— *Brown rice*: its bran is present, making it rich in fiber and vitamins.

— *Basmati rice*: its grain is long and thin. It remains whole and loose when cooked, and has a characteristic flavor. It is originally from India.

— *Jasmine rice*: it stands out for its jasmine aroma.

■ **Corn.** It has been consumed in America for at least 7,000 years. This cereal is very versatile in the kitchen. When fresh, corn on the cob can be eaten like a vegetable. The dried grains, on the other hand, can be eaten whole, crushed, or as flour. The latter is recommended for people with a compromised digestive system, sick people, and people who are allergic to gluten.

This is the only cereal that provides beta-carotene in very high doses, and it's rich in fiber, carbohydrates, iron, vitamin B1, and inositol, which is a form of vitamin B3 that helps regulate sleep and metabolizes fats.

Corn proteins (3 percent in fresh corn, 9 percent in dried corn) are better assimilated than wheat proteins. Corn is high in calories, making it beneficial in the diet of people who practice sports, and people with magnesium deficiency. Its high fiber content favors intestinal transit and reduces cholesterol. This is one of the most used ingredients in processed foods, used to make fructose, syrups, and modified starches.

Corn can be used to prepare a wide range of products, such as popcorn, which are much less nutritious than fresh corn or corn flour. If popcorn is going to be consumed, it's better to have the homemade variety, as commercial popcorn has unnecessary added fats. Corn is also consumed for breakfast in the form of flakes, which are also nutritionally poor, containing only carbohydrates and being high in calories, especially if they have added sugar.

Corn semolina can also be used to thicken soups or stews, just like polenta (corn flour with a relatively granulated texture that can be compacted), and it is a perfect ingredient to accompany fried or grilled vegetables, or to have with any sauce.

Corn oil is extracted from the grain's germ, but it's not very good for you from a health standpoint, as it is obtained through chemical procedures, it oxidizes easily because it's rich in polyunsaturated fatty acids, it's unstable when heated, and it doesn't keep the original nutritional properties of corn.

■ **Millet.** Very few people know that millet (*Panicum miliaceum*) was one of the first cereals ever grown. It has been a staple food in China and India for over 3,000 years, and today it is the main cereal for more than 400 million people. It's tasty, sweet, light, and alkalizing. It's also more nutritious, energy producing, and mineral-rich than the most used cereals. Strangely, in Spain it's very rarely consumed, and most people look down on it and consider it birds' food.

In dry areas, millet is a real solution for famines. It grows in poor soil, with little rain, and even when there is no rain at all the plants hibernate while they wait for the next rainy season. Millet can also be stored for many years.

Nutritionally speaking, it is very high in protein. Its proteins have a high biological value, and are more complete and more abundant than those in wheat, rice, and corn. It is the most energizing cereal, together with oatmeal. It's also high in iron, manganese, calcium, phosphorus, potassium, sodium, magnesium, zinc, and vitamins (A, B, and PP). Its levels of magnesium help absorb calcium. One of its components, silicic acid, explains why it stimulates the teeth enamel (this is proven by looking at the perfect teeth of Africans who consume large amounts of millet), and it also stimulates the hair, nails, skin, and intestinal tone (silicic acid helps contract the colon, and keeps it from swelling). Cosmetically, saline extracts of millet are produced, which help the hair shine and have body and bounce.

It's an energetic food, revitalizing, digestive, and diuretic; useful in the case of asthenia, anemia, and pregnancy (it prevents miscarriages and improves nutritional deficiencies). Its lecithin and choline content makes it ideal for weakened organisms, and for those who do lots of intellectual work. The natural medicine sector considers it to be an anti-stress food, and macrobiotics encourage its consumption due to its alkalizing properties, high content of iron and silicon, and its beneficial effect on the spleen, stomach, and pancreas.

Thanks to its versatility, millet has traditionally replaced rice in most recipes. Despite being gluten-free (and hence, recommended for people with celiac disease), it has a great binding power, as a result of its soluble fiber. This makes it a great ingredient to use in puddings and tarts, without having to add eggs or starch. Even though it is the sweetest cereal, it can easily adapt to savory dishes and desserts alike.

Other foods and gluten

Here we will share a list of both foods that contain gluten and foods that don't, even though nowadays the food industry offers a wide range of gluten-free alternatives to staple foods such as bread, muffins, pasta, etc., which normally contain gluten. These confections look very appetizing, but they also cost more, making a gluten-free diet more expensive (more on this later).

Types of foods

FOODS THAT CONTAIN GLUTEN
- Bread, wheat flour, barley, rye, and oatmeal.
- Muffins, pastries, tarts.
- Cookies, desserts.
- Pasta (spaghetti, macaroni, noodles).
- Milk shakes.
- Distilled or fermented drinks made from cereals: beer, whisky, barley water, some liquors.
- Any processed food that is made with any of the aforementioned flours in any of their forms: starch, semolina, protein, etc.

FOODS THAT MAY CONTAIN GLUTEN (it's better to avoid them or to make sure they don't have it)
- Processed meats: ham, sausages, etc.
- Charcuterie.
- Melted cheeses, spreading cheeses, and special cheeses for pizza.
- Flavored yogurt, with fruit pieces or marmalade.
- Pâtés, hamburgers, marinated meats.
- Meat preserves.

- Fish preserved in sauces.
- Candy.
- Coffee substitutes and other machine drinks, as it's hard to know if coffee has been mixed with malt.
- Dried fruits or toasted nuts, with or without salt.
- Some kinds of ice cream.
- Chocolate substitutes.
- Sauces, seasonings, and food dyes.

GLUTEN-FREE FOODS

- Milk and dairy: cheese, cottage cheese, cream, natural yogurt, curd.
- All kinds of meat and organ meats—fresh, frozen, naturally preserved, or dried.
- Fresh and frozen fish without a sauce, fresh seafood, and fish or seafood preserved in water or oil.
- Fresh, powdered, dehydrated, or liquid eggs.
- Vegetables and tubers.
- Fruits.
- Rice, corn, tapioca, and their derivatives.
- All kinds of legumes.
- Sugar and honey.
- Oils and butters.
- Coffee grains or ground coffee, herbal teas, and drinks.
- All kinds of wines and bubbly drinks.
- Dried fruits without additives (with or without salt).
- Salt, wine vinegar, fresh or ground spices.

As a general rule, all bulk products, artisan products, and products without proper labeling that shows a list of ingredients should be avoided.

Source: Celiac Disease Association of Madrid

What about additives? An additive is a substance that is added to food or beverages without trying to change its nutritional value, and with the purpose of extending its shelf life or of better adapting it to its desired use. These additives are numerated and always begin with the letter "E" (Europe). The only additives that can contain gluten are the modified starches (from E-1404 to E-1450).

Other than additives, there are also substances used to help incorporate the additive. In some cases, starch or bread crust is used with this purpose. When these "helpers" contain gluten, the manufacturer has to show it on the label.

An ingredient is any substance, including any additives, used in the preparation of any food, which is present in the final product. The ingredients that you can find in food labels that contain gluten are: gluten, cereals, flour, starch, modified starches (E-1404 to E-1450), fiber, thickeners, semolina, protein/vegetable protein, protein hydrolyzate/vegetable protein, malt, malt syrup, malt extract, yeast, yeast extract, and spices.

Following a gluten-free diet is not easy in Western countries, where wheat is the most consumed cereal, and the most used in processed foods, and where 70 percent to 80 percent of the products found in a supermarket contain gluten. This ingredient is used in the food industry as an additive excipient, to preserve humidity, to block fat, as an aroma excipient, to avoid oxidation, etc.

A gluten-free diet is challenging both for the people following it and for their families (especially in the case of children), and also for dietitians and doctors, as there are many ways in which the person can ingest gluten without knowing it.

■ The most important thing for a person with celiac disease is to follow a very strict diet, which should consist mostly of fresh and natural products that don't contain gluten in their natural state: meats, fish, eggs, fruits, vegetables, legumes, and permitted cereals (corn and rice), making sure to combine them in varied and well-balanced ways.

- The biggest risk for people following this diet comes when they consume processed foods. These should be avoided as much as possible, as it's hard to know if they truly are gluten-free. There is always the possibility that gluten was added as an ingredient, as an additive, or that it got in during the manufacturing process.

- In the same way, all bulk products, artisanal products, and products that aren't properly labeled should be avoided, because it's hard to confirm all their ingredients. When in doubt, it's better to avoid it.

- When buying processed foods, the list of ingredients on the label should always be read. Anything containing wheat, barley, rye, oatmeal, and anything derived from these should be avoided: flours, starches, proteins, malts, thickeners, etc. However, checking the label is not a complete guarantee anymore, as the law today doesn't force the labeling of the botanical origin of flours, starches, semolina, or other derivatives from wheat, oatmeal, barley, rye, or triticale.

BE CAREFUL OF ANY CROSS-CONTAMINATION

When cooking food for a person with celiac disease, there are some rules that should be followed to make sure no contamination with gluten takes place:

— Don't touch foods containing gluten, and then the gluten-free foods.
— Don't use the oil in which foods with gluten have been fried (empanadas, croquettes, etc.) to fry gluten-free foods.

— Don't use the same cutlery that has touched any butters, marmalades, mayonnaise, etc.
— Carefully wash all the kitchen utensils, glasses, dishes, cutlery, and cookware, so no trace of gluten is left.
— If a dish (for example, some pasta) is prepared in its gluten and gluten-free versions, make sure you keep them completely separate from each other: use different utensils, pans, strainers, etc.
— Keep the allowed foods separate from the rest.
— The families of people with celiac disease should use gluten-free breads and flours if possible, to avoid any cross-contamination.

Other recommendations

Supplements and phytotherapy

Diet is the main and only treatment of celiac disease. However, the use of several natural resources can help enhance the patient's health. These remedies are only helpful as a complement to a gluten-free diet, and under supervision of a dietitian or doctor.

- **Multivitamins:** People with celiac disease tend to have a deficiency of several vitamins, which is why a multivitamin could help bring them back to normal levels. They usually contain vitamin D, which is necessary for the correct absorption of calcium, and for bone health in general. These kinds of vitamins are also beneficial for those patients who also suffer from lactose intolerance.

- **Phytotherapy:** People with celiac disease can use plants with demulcent properties, which have a high content of mucilages, to make the lining of the gut softer.

If these are taken, it must be done under medical supervision. The reason for this is that these treatments can sometimes counteract with other prescribed medications, or react with the patient's sensitive gut, having negative effects.

- **Chamomile (*Matricaria chamomilla*):** It has anti-inflammatory and relaxing properties that can alleviate any inflammations, prevent swelling, and lower any pain. At the same time, its healing properties can make any lesion in the intestinal wall milder. Drinking two cups a day of the infusion of one tablespoon of dried flowers per cup of water is recommended.

- **Marshmallow (*Althaea officinalis*):** Its richness in mucilages makes it the perfect treatment for irritated membranes. The presence of tannins can help stop the frequency of bowel movements. It can be prepared as an infusion of one teaspoon of flowers and dried leaves per cup of water (let them infuse for 10 minutes). Take two cups per day.

Tips for outside the home

- **At school:** In the case of children, it's important to give the office, teachers, and people responsible for food preparation notice of your child's celiac disease. If the food is provided by an out-of-school catering company, make sure they know about this disease as well. Knowing if there's another child suffering from celiac disease in the same school is useful, as well as knowing if there's a person in charge of supervising the children while they eat. It's helpful if the teacher informs the other students of the child's intolerance, to avoid being rejected, and to give the teacher candy, cookies, and other gluten-free treats if there's a birthday party or any other celebration.

- **In bars and restaurants:** It's important to tell the waiter what foods need to be avoided. A good option at restaurants are salads (without dressing), grilled meat or fish with a side of grilled vegetables (without sauces, creams, or French fries), and for dessert, natural fruit or natural juice shouldn't be a problem. At a bar, good snack options are a plate of cheese and meat, grilled calamari, or steamed mussels, for example.

- **When traveling:** It's advisable to contact the celiac association of the area you're traveling to in advance, to be informed of the places where gluten-free products can be found. There's also an increasing number of hotels and hostels that include gluten-free foods on their menus. However, the best choice is to rent an apartment, where you can prepare your own food.

    When traveling by plane you can order a gluten-free menu at the time of purchasing your ticket, and most airlines cater to this special diet. It's advisable to find out if the airline provides this kind of food before buying a ticket. GFML (*gluten-free meal*) is the acronym that identifies this special menu in an airline.

    Traveling on a cruise can also be a valid option if you have celiac disease. Some companies offer a gluten-free menu to people who request it. Just make sure you request it a week or two in advance.

    Even if you follow this advice, it's always wise to contact the celiac associations of each state or country, as they will be able to tell you where you can get the best food for your condition.

PAY ATTENTION TO MEDICATIONS

Pharmaceutical products could contain gluten, flours, starches, or other derivatives in their preparation. In July 12, 1989, the General Direction of Health and Pharmacy (BOE number 179), gave a resolution under which gluten must be labeled as part of the components of pharmacological substances. This resolution became active in 1991, so all the medications since then follow this rule, and people can know if they contain gluten or not. However, when in doubt, it's better to ask a doctor or pharmacist.

The Center of Medication Information provides any kind of information required about medications (whether they contain gluten, a description of components, etc.).

More Tips

- Having a healthy lifestyle, sleeping enough, practicing some kind of exercise, and avoiding emotional stress as much as possible are habits that keep health at optimal levels.
- Attending meetings of people with the same problem helps you to share different experiences and expand your knowledge about the disease.
- Try to learn more about the disease: go to talks or informative sessions that are organized in your community, offering new facts or perspectives about the disease: treatment, diet, psychological supports, and other topics of interest.
- Get into the habit of regularly inquiring about the ingredients of processed or packaged foods to avoid those that may cause damage.
- Get a list of gluten-free foods. This can be requested from food manufacturers.
- Get in touch with groups of people affected by the same disease, or celiac disease associations to get the needed help and support.
- Find a nutritionist to help you create appropriate menus, and know which foods in the market are safe.

Gluten-free products

On top of the dietary recommendations we've given, and the possible natural remedies to help improve the symptoms, those suffering from this disease can consume products that are made without gluten.

Celiac associations in different communities provide lists of processed products (such as cooked ham, tomato sauce, cured meats, etc.) which can be consumed without danger because they don't contain gluten.

According to the Spanish Federation of Celiac Associations (FACE), 80 percent of processed foods are not safe for people with celiac disease, and even worse, labels don't always make it clear if they contain gluten or not. However, in 2006 there were already 1,100 processed foods made specifically gluten-free, a number which is much higher nowadays.

Limiting gluten

The FAO/OMS Commission of the Codex Alimentarius was created in 1962 in Rome by the United Nations Organization for Food and Agriculture (FAO), and the World Health Organization

(WHO), with the aim of creating a joint program of dietary guidelines. Its acronym is ALINORM.

In the twentieth meeting of this commission (Bonn, 1996), it was established that the limit of gluten that a food labeled as "gluten-free" could contain was 200 ppm (parts per million = 200 mg of gluten / 1 kg product). However, in the twenty-second reunion (Geneva, 1997), the need to lower this to 20 ppm (20 mg of gluten / 1 kg product) was discussed.

These limits are what would be permitted from a legal standpoint. However, the limit tolerated by people with celiac disease is still unknown, which is the reason why their consumption should be as low as zero to avoid future complications and unnecessary problems. Consuming it and not showing any symptoms doesn't mean that the body is tolerating it, as it's been proven that tiny amounts of gluten can severely damage the villi, or cause alterations in the gut.

FACE had established 2006 as the deadline to reduce this number to 20 ppm, and it has since been lowered it to 10 ppm. For this reason, it created its guaranteed label "Controlled by FACE." In this way, a person with celiac disease who acquires a product with this label can be certain that it's safe.

WHAT DOES THE "CONTROLLED BY FACE" LABEL MEAN?

This label establishes whether or not a product has complied with the requirements established by FACE about the maximum levels of gluten. Accredited laboratories test these products using studies that guarantee that they are safe for consumption by celiac people.

The federation signs an agreement with the food manufacturers that request it, and they commit to guarantee that their products have less than 10 ppm of gluten. FACE closely follows the products where gluten is detected and warns all its associates until the situation is corrected. Thanks to this practice, people with celiac disease who buy products with this label can be sure that they are safe. This organization also informs all the European celiac disease associations about the meaning of the label "controlled by FACE."

What does the crossed-out grain sign mean?

A crossed-out grain inside a circle is an international "gluten-free" symbol. It was designed by Michael Carpenter, who transferred the copyright to the United Kingdom's Celiac Society, the entity that owns the right to control its use.

During the AOECS congress in Zeist (June 1989), the United Kingdom's Celiac Society made each country's celiac associations responsible for guaranteeing the proper use of this sign. As a result, many products that are allowed in a gluten-free diet can be easily identified by carrying this international gluten-free food symbol.

This sign, however, doesn't guarantee the complete absence of gluten. It just guarantees that the product that has it follows the Codex Alimentarius standard.

FACE is the national proprietor of this symbol, and the one responsible for allowing its use in publications and activities organized by several celiac associations. In Spain, the government doesn't perform systematic controls of the products in the market, whether they are labeled "gluten-free" or carry this symbol, or any of the variations created by the companies. Food companies use these labels freely without authorization, and in many cases even without testing the products periodically to prove that they are free from gluten.

When traveling abroad, or buying foreign gluten-free products that carry this symbol, it should be known that they may contain gluten, as some European celiac associations accept the Codex guidelines, which consider a product "gluten-free" if they contain up to the Codex Alimentarius standard amount of gluten.

Patients who buy products with the label "controlled by FACE" have a greater guarantee. This label indicates that the product has been tested regularly to detect gluten. FACE signs an agreement with the companies that request it, and they commit to paying for the costs of these tests, and to remove any batches that come out positive for gluten from the market.

Detecting gluten

At present, there is an international group of experts (Working Group on Prolamin) that works together to find new testing methods for gluten which will show the exact amount of gluten in the products. This is a vital advance, considering that today, the only treatment available for people with celiac disease is to follow a strict gluten-free diet.

In Spain, the Gluten Unit of the National Biotechnology center (Universidad Autónoma de Madrid) has become in recent years a reference point for gluten-free testing across Europe. The techniques that are being developed to detect gluten are:

- **Immunological techniques:** Sandwich ELISA-R5 to detect gluten from wheat, barley, and rye; competitive and sandwich ELISA to detect oatmeal; competitive ELISA-R5 to detect hydrolyzed gluten; and Western Blot-R5 to detect wheat, barley, and rye, and to confirm the results provided by the ELISA.

- **Non-immunological techniques:** MALDI-TOF mass spectrometry, to detect prolamins from wheat, barley, rye, and oatmeal, and to confirm the results given by ELISA. PCR to detect wheat DNA, and to confirm the results of ELISA and of a gluten extraction cocktail.

■ **Testing techniques for celiac disease:** Quick immunochromatographic strips to screen celiac disease in two formats: simple strips that detect anti-transglutaminase tissue (t-TG), and another kind of double strips that detect anti-transglutaminase tissue (t-TG) and anti-gliadin antibodies (AGA) simultaneously.

All these techniques are still being studied.

An expensive disease

Taking into account that 80 percent of the products in the market contain gluten (processed meats, nougats, chocolates, sauces, mayonnaise, dairy desserts, seasonings, and more), and that consuming even the slightest portion of this protein can cause significant undesirable consequences (even if the person with celiac disease is not aware of these consequences), the Celiac Association of Madrid has done studies calculating the cereal consumption of a person suffering from celiac disease according to the Spanish Society of Community Nutrition for the Spanish population, to get an estimate of the cost. The results show that following a gluten-free diet represents an extraordinary extra cost in food of $152 (122.2 euros) per month, which would add up to $1,821 (1,466.4 euros) per year.

People who can afford this extra cost don't get any kind of government help, nor funding from any other public or private institution that could help them meet this cost. This is different in most other countries in the European Union, among them

Austria, Italy, Ireland, Finland, France, Norway, Portugal, United Kingdom, Switzerland, etc. Only a few public and private organizations give their workers a little economic help.

Comparative study of the price of regular and gluten-free products, 2008. Source: Celiac Association of Madrid.

Product (2.2 pounds)	With gluten (euros)	Without gluten (euros)
Flour	0.4	7.6
Sliced bread	1.3	16.2
Toasted bread	2.2	3.3
Grated bread	0.4	16.2
Pasta	1.2	18
Noodles	0.9	13
Pizza base	1.6	21.1
Cookies	1.2	22.4
Chocolate cookies	2.6	32.6
Cake	2.8	26.7
Madeleines	1.8	20.8
Chocolate muffins	3.5	35
Baguette	2.3	25.5
Breakfast Cereal	2.1	15.4

Despite the price, there's an increasing number of gluten-free products in the market, which has made the life of those intolerant to this protein much easier. Even foods considered treats have now gluten-free versions to satisfy the cravings of those who suffer from this condition and their families:

■ **Campaign for gluten-free candy.** Another improvement for celiac children in Spain is the campaign led by the Celiac

Association of Cataluña, with the goal of including gluten-free candy during the religious celebrations.

Many town halls approved this request, such as the one in Sant Joan Despí, which gave away around 7,700 pounds (3,500 kilos) of candy, half of them without gluten. With this initiative, this town hall wanted to address the request of a family in that town who had a gluten-free child.

- **Gluten-free beer.** In 2006, Damm was the first Spanish company to sell a barley beer in Spain, which has low levels of gluten and can be consumed by people with celiac disease. This was great news for this region, because until then, they considered drinking beer to be an impossible dream due to their chronic intestinal disease.

  This beer has the same taste as regular beer and six gluten particles per million. The international code stated that 20 gluten particles are the allowed limit for a person who is intolerant to gluten. Regular beers have an average of 150, 250, and even 3,000 gluten particles in some German and Belgian beers.

  Now, many brands sell gluten-free beers.

ARGUMENTS WITH THE CHURCH

Despite having come a long way, there are still some obstacles for people with celiac disease. One of these was what happened in a town in Aragon, Spain, in 2008. There, the parents of a celiac boy asked the church if he could take Holy Communion with a corn host, instead of one made with wheat, as the latter would be dangerous for the boy's health. They were unpleasantly surprised when the priest of Santiago Church, in the capital of Aragon, and then José Antonio Satué, vicar of the Huesca Diocesis, denied this request, even though the host was going to be provided by the Celiac Association.

They were told that as an alternative, their son could take the communion with wine, but the boy's parents were opposed to their son drinking alcohol, and this was also against the law. They proposed to change this suggestion to drinking grape juice, but the vicar insisted that it had to be wine. Europa Press reported that the church defended itself by stating that these are universal traditions that they don't have the power to change, without exceptions.

.

Cooking without gluten

Most cookbooks contain recipes that don't fit a gluten-free diet. So what can a person suffering from celiac disease do?

It is true that the dishes prepared in most cookbooks, and the products sold in most stores, can't be consumed by this group of people due to one or more of the ingredients they contain. However, in most cases, recipes can be easily modified. Here are two examples: if the recipe calls for one cup of wheat flour, this can be replaced with one cup of wheat starch, one cup of corn flour, one cup of finely ground corn flour, three-quarters cup of coarse corn flour, ten tablespoons of potato starch, fourteen tablespoons of rice flour, one cup of soy flour plus a quarter cup of potato starch, or half a cup of soy flour plus half a cup of potato starch.

Also, sauces that are thickened with a tablespoon of wheat flour can be thickened with a tablespoon of corn starch, potato starch, rice starch, or arrowroot. You can also do this using two tablespoons of easy-cook tapioca. In any event, it's not hard to find cookbooks specifically created for gluten-free cooking.

Some advice

■ Always favor cooking techniques that use less fat: with water—boiled, steamed, or poached—sautéed, grilled, roasted, or baked in foil or parchment.

■ Consume foods that have been fried, dipped in egg and corn flour batter, and stews, in moderation. In the case of stews, remove the fat once it's cool, as this makes it easier to store and makes it more nutritious.

■ Limit the amount of fats you use to dress your food: oils, butter, margarines, cream, lard, homemade mayonnaise, sauces with eggs, cheese, milk, and other greasy ingredients.

■ Several herbs and spices can be used to make the food more flavorful: basil, fennel, cumin, cayenne pepper, bay leaves, thyme, oregano, parsley, marjoram, pepper, or saffron.

■ Wine and apple vinegar, and olive and seed oils, can be macerated with aromatic herbs.

■ Use different utensils to stir and serve the food of a celiac person than the ones you use for the rest of the family.

■ Don't cut any gluten-free bread with the same knife you use for regular bread. Don't use the same chopping board or dish either. The same advice applies when dipping a knife in butter or marmalade when you are using them to spread a regular bread, because some tiny crumbs will stay in them.

■ Be careful not to use oil that has previously been used to fry croquettes, calamari, or any fried food containing wheat flour.

Tip: Always put a label on the previously used oil that you plan on using again, so you know what has been cooked in it before.

- Cleaning the oven, where both foods with gluten and foods without gluten are usually cooked, is extremely important. It's helpful to clean it well, and to be careful that you don't bake foods with gluten and foods without gluten at the same time.

- When you prepare a recipe using canned foods, and then store it in a glass jar, always put on a label stating what brands of canned products were used.

- Freeze your gluten-free foods in individual containers, and always put a label on them so you can identify them.

Recipe Substitutions

You can replace one cup of wheat flour with:
- 1 cup corn flour
- 1 cup finely ground corn flour
- ¾ cup coarse corn flour
- 10 tablespoons potato starch
- 14 tablespoons rice flour
- 1 cup soy flour, plus ¼ cup potato starch
- ½ cup soy flour, plus ½ cup potato starch

For recipes

Eating gluten-free doesn't equal eating only half of the foods available. There are plenty of foods that are free from gluten, and the market is filled with products that are specific for a gluten-free diet. Celiac disease associations regularly release lists of products made and packaged safely, and they also give cooking classes. Here we will show you how being celiac doesn't mean having to stop eating many delightful foods such as bread, tarts, and cakes. Thanks to many effective and delicious alternative ingredients, we can enjoy all of these foods in their gluten-free versions. On top of this, we will share several appetizers and entrees, which you will be able to cook without worry, and which will also help you look like a star in the kitchen.

Note: Where it's not specified, recipes are written for 4-5 portions.

1. Basic Recipes

SAUCES
Many ready-made sauces have gluten as one of their ingredients. However, you don't have to live without them, because here we'll tell you how to make the basic cooking sauces at home. This way, you won't miss a recipe.

Aiolo
Ingredients:
- 3 garlic cloves
- 1 teaspoon kosher salt
- 1 large egg yolk
- 1 teaspoon lemon juice
- black pepper
- ½ cups olive oil (*not* extra virgin)

Method:

In a mortar, crush the garlic with a teaspoon of kosher salt until a paste consistency is achieved. Incorporate the egg yolk and lemon juice until combined. Starting slowly, add a few drops of oil at a time while mixing quickly. Continue to add the oil until the mixture is thick and creamy.

Season with black pepper and additional salt and lemon juice if needed.

Tomato Sauce

Ingredients:

- 2 lb ripe plum tomatoes (peeled, cored, and seeded)
- 1 cup chopped Spanish onion
- 4 cloves chopped garlic
- ¼ cup olive oil
- 2 dry bay leaves
- salt
- 2 teaspoons sherry vinegar

Method:

Puree the tomatoes in a food processor or crush them as finely as possible in a bowl with your hands.

In a medium-sized saucepan, heat the olive oil over medium-low heat. Add the onions, garlic, bay leaves, and a pinch of salt; stir and turn the heat to low.

Gently cook the vegetables until soft and tender. Add the tomatoes and heat to a simmer. Simmer the sauce over medium-low heat, stirring fairly often for about 1 hour. Once thickened, remove the bay leaves and season with the vinegar and salt to taste.

Mayonnaise

Ingredients:

- 1 egg yolk
- ½ teaspoon Dijon mustard

- ¾ cup olive oil (*not* extra virgin)
- 1 tablespoon lemon juice
- salt

Method:

In a food processor, add the egg yolk, mustard, and lemon juice and combine. Starting slowly, add a few drops of oil while the processor is running. Continue to add the oil in a steady stream until the mixture is thick and creamy.

Season with lemon juice and salt to taste.

Tofu Mayonnaise

Ingredients:

- 1 ¼ cups silken tofu
- 1 tablespoon white miso
- 2 tablespoons vegetable oil
- 1 tablespoon lemon juice
- salt

Method:

Chop the tofu into small pieces and place in a strainer so the excess liquid will drain off. Let the tofu strain for 1 hour.

In a food processor, add the tofu, miso, and lemon juice and pulse until smooth mixture is formed. Starting slowly, add a few drops of oil while the processor is running. Continue to add the oil in steady stream until the mixture is thick and creamy.

Season with salt to taste.

Romesco Sauce

Ingredients:

- 2 large tomatoes (peeled, seeded, and chopped)
- 2 garlic cloves
- 1 dried ancho chile pepper
- 2 tablespoons blanched almonds

- 2 tablespoons hazelnuts (skinned and toasted)
- ¼ cup drained bottled pimientos (rinsed)
- 1 teaspoon apple cider vinegar
- extra virgin olive oil

Method·

Place the ancho chile in a small saucepan and cover with water. Bring to a simmer over high heat and pull off the flame. Let soak for at least 30 minutes. Remove the chile once softened and let cool.

Heat a medium sauté pan over moderate heat with a thin layer of oil. Once hot, add the hazelnuts, almonds, and garlic, stirring until everything is toasted and fragrant, about 3 minutes. Transfer entire contents to a bowl.

Remove the seeds and stem from the chile and coarsely chop the flesh. Add to a food processor along with the tomatoes, nuts, garlic, pimientos, and vinegar.

Puree until smooth. Adjust consistency with olive oil and season with salt.

DOUGH

Pizza

Ingredients:

- 2 cups (200 g) rice flour
- 2 teaspoons instant dry yeast (10 g)
- ¾ cup (20 cl) warm water
- ⅛ teaspoon (1 g) salt

Method:

In a small bowl, combine yeast and warm water. Make sure it's not too hot, or it will kill the yeast. Let sit for 5 minutes to activate.

Mix the flour and salt. Add the water and yeast mixture and mix quickly. Once combined, use a spatula to spread the dough on a large sheet pan sprayed with non-stick cooking spray, until it's about half an inch thick.

Bake for 10 minutes at 375°F. Remove shell from the oven, cover with a thin layer of tomato sauce and toppings of your choice, without getting too close to the edges.

Variation

Put it back in the oven and bake for 15 minutes.

Ingredients:
- 3 ¼ cups (400 g) cornstarch
- 1 cup (100 g) corn flour
- 3 tablespoons (30 g) fresh yeast
- 2 cups (½ l) warm water
- ½ teaspoon salt

Method:

In a small bowl, combine the yeast and warm water. Not too hot or it will kill the yeast. Let sit for 5 minutes to activate.

Mix the corn flour, cornstarch, and salt. Add the water and yeast mixture and combine to form a dough. Knead the dough with your hands just until a ball can be formed. Place in a bowl, cover in plastic wrap, and let rest at room temperature for 2 hours.

Once rested, use your hands to stretch the dough on a large sheet pan sprayed with non-stick cooking spray. Cover with a thin layer of tomato sauce and toppings of your choice, without getting too close to the edges.

Bake at 375°F for 20 minutes.

FOR PIE

This pie dough is very easy to make and has a taste that goes well with savory filling, all kinds of quiches, or vegetable tarts.

Ingredients:

- 1 cup (100 g) quinoa flour
- 1 cup (100 g) rice flour
- 1 teaspoon salt
- 1 teaspoon active dry yeast
- 2 eggs
- 4 tablespoons olive oil

Method:

In a small bowl, combine the yeast and 2 tablespoons of warm water. Make sure the water is not too hot, or it will kill the yeast. Let sit for 5 minutes to activate the yeast.

Put all the dry ingredients in the bowl of a mixer. Mix them well and add 1 or 2 tablespoons water, until the dough starts to come together. Add the olive oil and eggs and mix until a ball is formed.

Remove from mixer and knead lightly and put on the kitchen counter, dusted with rice flour. With a floured rolling pin, flatten the dough to ⅛ inch in thickness.

Line the pie pan with the dough and cut away the excess. Fill the shell with filling of your choice or pre-bake and reserve.

GLUTEN-FREE PASTA

Ingredients:

- 2 cups (250 g) cornstarch
- 1 cup (100 g) corn flour
- 4 eggs and one egg white
- 1 teaspoon olive oil
- 1 teaspoon salt
- A little bit of water

Method:

Sift the cornstarch, corn flour, and salt through a strainer. Form a mound with the flour and make a well in the center.

Put the eggs, egg white, and olive oil in it. Mix everything well, until the dough comes together. Knead lightly until a ball is formed.

Dust some cornstarch over the kitchen counter and knead the dough with your hands for 10 minutes. The dough should become smooth and uniform in texture. Wrap it up with plastic wrap and refrigerate for 10 minutes. Flatten the dough with a rolling pin, forming a very thin rectangle.

With a knife, portion the dough into desired shape.

FOR STUFFED PASTRIES

Ingredients:

- 3 ½ cups (500 g) gluten-free flour
- 1 ½ teaspoons (10 g) salt
- 1 package active dry yeast
- ½ cup (100 g) olive oil
- 1 cup (200 cc) water

Method:

Combine flour, yeast, olive oil, and water together in the bowl. Work the mixture until you can form a dough. Knead it on a floured counter until it comes together into a uniform mass. Continue to knead it until it becomes a smooth and elastic dough. Shape it into a ball and let it rest for 20 minutes. After, divide the ball in two equal parts, and flatten each with a floured rolling pin until you get an extremely thin sheet.

Fill the center with a filling of your choice. Fold over the dough, seam to seam, to cover the filling. Bake at 375°F for 8–12 minutes.

FOR PUFF PASTRY

Ingredients:

- 4 ¼ cups (600 g) gluten-free flour
- 1 cup + 1 tablespoon (250 ml) warm milk

- 1 cup + 1 tablespoon (250 ml) warm water
- 1 ½ teaspoons (10 g) salt
- 2 teaspoons (10 g) sugar
- 1 ⅓ cup (300 g) soft margarine

Method:

In the bowl of a stand mixer, combine the margarine with ⅓ cup (50 g) of flour. Let mix until the flour is fully incorporated and the mixture has softened.

On a parchment-lined sheet tray, spread the butter mixture into a 2-inch thick rectangle and place into the freezer to set.

In a medium saucepan, combine the water, milk, salt, and sugar. Warm gently over low heat.

On your kitchen counter, mound up the remaining flour and make a hole in the center. Gently pour the water, milk, salt, and sugar in it. Mix everything and knead vigorously until you get smooth dough.

Use a rolling pin to extend the dough into a large rectangle that is about half an inch thick.

Place the margarine and flour rectangle in the center and fold the dough over once and press against the margarine. Roll the dough again, carefully forming a rectangle that is half an inch thick. Continue to repeat the process until you have folded the dough in half four times.

Wrap the dough in plastic wrap and let rest in the refrigerator for 20 minutes before using as desired.

2. Soups

TOMATO AND CORN SOUP

Ingredients:

- 3 cups (¾ l) vegetable stock
- 1 ½ lbs (750 g) ripe tomatoes

- 2 cups (200 g) corn flour
- 2 tablespoons oil
- 1 bay leaf
- 1 teaspoon (2 g) dry oregano
- 1 teaspoon (2 g) dry basil
- Salt
- Pepper

Method:

Peel, seed, and crush the tomatoes. Add one tablespoon of olive oil to a medium-sized saucepan and heat over medium-low heat. Add the tomatoes and sauté for 10 minutes, along with the bay leaf, oregano, basil, and pepper.

In a blender, add the vegetable stock and corn flour and blend on high until the flour is dissolved, adding more stock if necessary.

Pour the thickened vegetable stock into a medium sauce pan and bring to a simmer over medium heat, stirring frequently.

Once the tomatoes are thickened, remove the bay leaf and add the tomatoes to the soup.

Cook over low heat for 5 more minutes. Add salt to taste and serve.

CHINESE SOUP

Ingredients:

- 6 cups (1 ½ l) chicken stock
- 4 green onions (white and green part)
- 4 ripe tomatoes
- ¾ oz (20 g) Chinese soy noodles
- 2 eggs
- 2 pinches ground ginger
- 4 teaspoons sesame seeds
- gluten-free soy sauce

Method:

Soak the noodles in warm water for 14 minutes before you start cooking.

Blanch, peel, and seed, and chop the tomatoes. Slice the green onions.

Heat a large saucepot over medium heat. Add 1 tablespoon of vegetable oil to the pan and sauté the green onions. When they are soft, add the sesame seeds, tomato, ginger, and gluten-free soy sauce. Cook for 5 minutes.

Strain the noodles and add them to the pan. Add the stock and bring to a simmer. Cook for 5 to 10 minutes.

Beat the eggs. While stirring, add them to the boiling soup.

Turn the heat off while you wait for the eggs to thicken and float.

Serve with soy sauce, toasted sesame seeds, and a sprinkling of chopped green onion.

3. Salads and other Appetizers

ZUCCHINI WITH EGGS, HIJIKI, AND OLIVES
Ingredients:

- 1 large zucchini
- 6 eggs (beaten)
- ¾ lb (400 g) ripe tomatoes
- ¼ cup (50 g) green olives
- 2 tablespoons dried hijiki seaweed
- 2 garlic cloves
- 3 tablespoons (50 ml) extra virgin olive oil
- Basil leaves
- Parsley leaves
- salt
- a pinch of brown sugar
- a pinch of herbal

Method:

Soak the seaweed in cold water for 15 minutes to hydrate. Strain and add to a pot large enough to cover the seaweed with water completely. Bring to a simmer and let cook for 15 minutes. Strain and set aside.

Wash the zucchini and cut lengthwise into thin ribbons. Blanch in boiling water for 1 minute and transfer to a bowl of ice water. Once cool, remove the ribbons and place them on layers of paper towels to dry completely. Set aside.

Peel and thinly slice the garlic. Peel and deseed the tomatoes and cut into cubes. Heat 2 tablespoons oil in a pan over low heat; add the garlic and tomatoes and a couple leaves of basil and parsley. Season the mixture with brown sugar and salt to taste. Cook over low heat for 15 minutes.

Chop the olives and mix them with the seaweed and the eggs. Heat 3 tablespoons of olive oil in a pan, pour the ingredients in the pan, season with salt and the herbs and stir until the eggs cook and thicken. Set aside.

Lay out the zucchini slices individually and place a teaspoon of the scrambled eggs at one end of each slice. Roll each slice gently to encase the scrambled eggs with the zucchini.

Place the tomatoes at the bottom of each plate using a round metal ring to shape them nicely. Place two zucchini rolls on top.

QUINOA, CHICORY, AND FENUGREEK SPROUTS

Ingredients:

- ⅔ cup (50 g) fenugreek sprouts (you can also use alfalfa, watercress, or onion sprouts)
- 3 cups (¼ kg) cooked quinoa
- 1 small bunch chicory leaves
- 1 ripe tomato
- 1 small onion

- 1 tablespoon extra-virgin olive oil
- Fresh oregano leaves

For the dressing:

- 2 zucchini
- 1 clove peeled garlic
- 3 tablespoons spiced oil
- sea salt

Method

To make the dressing, steam the zucchini with the garlic then mash them with salt. Let the mixture cool completely. Add the oil and spices and mix well.

Peel and deseed the tomato, then cut it in small cubes. Peel the onion, cut it in small cubes, and mix with the tomato cubes. Add the oil and oregano leaves and macerate for half an hour.

Mix the cooked quinoa with the zucchini dressing in a bowl.

To serve, break off a few chicory leaves and place them on each dish. Cover with the quinoa and the sprouts on top. Surround the salad with the macerated tomato and onion.

GREEN BEAN SALAD WITH CAULIFLOWER AND POTATO

Ingredients:

- 3 cups (½ k) green beans
- 2 cups (¼ k) cauliflower
- 1 ½ cups (350 g) potatoes
- ¼ cup (25 g) pine nuts
- ½ cup (50 g) watercress
- 1 sheet of nori
- 2 garlic cloves, chopped
- ¼ teaspoon paprika
- Lemon juice
- Extra virgin olive oil
- salt

Method:

To make the sauce, sauté the garlic cloves in 3 tablespoon olive oil over low heat for 5 minutes. Season the garlic oil with the paprika and salt to taste. When the oil is cool, add 2 tablespoons of lemon juice and reserve.

Heat a dry pan and toast the nori sheet until it becomes aromatic. Once cooled, break into small pieces and reserve.

To make the salad, wash the green beans and the cauliflower with plenty of fresh water, then cut into pieces. Peel and cut the potatoes into equally sized pieces. Steam these three vegetables until they are tender.

Once everything has cooled, toss the cooked vegetables with the watercress, pine nuts, and the dressing. Garnish with the toasted nori and serve.

ASIAN SALAD

Ingredients:
- 10 oz (375 g) Chinese rice noodles
- 2 cups (300 g) firm tofu
- 2 onions
- 1 cucumber
- 2 cups (150 g) bean sprouts
- 1 red bell pepper
- 1 tablespoon chopped parsley
- 1 large bunch chard leaves

For the dressing:
- 2 tablespoons gluten-free soy sauce
- zest of 1 lemon
- 1 minced garlic clove
- 1 tablespoon brown sugar
- 2 tablespoons oil

Method:

Wash the chard leaves well and blanch them in boiling water. Shock the leaves in a large bowl of ice water. Drain them.

In the meantime, finely chop the onions. Cut the tofu in cubes (be careful not to crumble it). Cut the cucumber in half, remove the seeds, and cut it in very thin diagonal slices. Cut the pepper in small cubes. Coarsely chop the parsley. Make the dressing by whisking together all its ingredients.

Put the Chinese noodles in a heat-resistant bowl, and cover with boiling water. Let them cook for 10 minutes, drain, rinse with cold water. Drain well and transfer to a large bowl. Mix all the ingredients together in the salad bowl and add the dressing right before serving.

CHICKPEAS WITH MINT

Ingredients:

- 1 ¾ (200 g) cups Bocconcini mozzarella cheese
- 1 ⅓ cups (350 g) cooked chickpeas
- 1 bunch escarole
- 4 ripe tomatoes
- 10 leaves fresh mint
- 1-2 tablespoons balsamic vinegar
- extra virgin olive oil
- salt

Method:

Toss the mozzarella balls with the mint leaves, olive oil, and a pinch of salt. Marinate for 10 minutes. Wash the escarole under cold water. Remove the thick stems and cut the leaves into smaller pieces.

Wash and cut the tomatoes, remove the seeds, and cut in small cubes. Toss the chickpeas with the vinegar, oil, and salt.

Combine the tomato with the dressed chickpeas. Arrange the escarole and mozzarella cheese on a serving platter and top with the chick pea mixture.

BUCKWHEAT WITH SWEET VEGETABLES

Ingredients:
- 1 cup raw buckwheat
- 2 onions, diced
- 1 cup pumpkin, diced
- 2 carrots, thinly sliced
- 3 tablespoons cooked corn
- olive oil
- 1 teaspoon sea salt
- 3 ½ cups water
- 1 bay leaf
- 1 tablespoon capers
- chopped parsley

Method:

Wash the buckwheat and drain well. Toast it in a dry skillet for a few minutes until it is dry and takes on a golden color.

In a medium saucepan, sauté the onions with olive oil and a pinch of sea salt for 10 minutes over medium-low heat.

Add the carrot, pumpkin, corn, buckwheat, 1 teaspoon sea salt, and 3 ½ cups water. Put the lid on and bring to a boil. Turn the heat to low and cook for 25 minutes or until the liquid has evaporated. Finally, garnish with the capers and parsley, and serve.

BELL PEPPER AND OLIVE QUICHE

Ingredients:
- 2 pieces fresh tofu
- 3 onions
- 2 bell peppers, (seeded, washed, and finely sliced)

- ½ cup (100 g) pitted olives
- 5 tablespoons (60 g) white miso
- 2 tablespoons water
- 2 tablespoons olive oil
- pinch of turmeric
- fresh basil
- pinch of dried basil
- pinch of sea salt

Method:

In a medium sauté pan, cook the onions with a bit of olive oil and a pinch of sea salt for 10 minutes. Add the sliced bell pepper and a bit of dried basil to your taste.

Place the tofu in a blender with the water, white miso, turmeric, and 2 tablespoons olive oil, and process until thick like custard.

Combine the tofu cream with the vegetables, olives, and fresh basil in a baking pan.

Bake at 375°F for 45 minutes. Cool, slice, and serve with more fresh basil as garnish.

4. Entrees

COLD CHICKPEA CROQUETTES WITH SESAME SEEDS

Ingredients:

- 2 ½ cups cooked chickpeas
- 2 carrots, peeled and grated
- ½ cup (65 g) breadcrumbs
- ½ teaspoon ground cumin
- 1 tablespoon chopped cilantro or parsley
- 1 tablespoon olive oil
- 1 ⅓ cups (200 g) sesame seeds, lightly toasted
- 2 teaspoons salt

Method:

Warm the chickpeas in a saucepan with enough water to cover them for 10 minutes. Drain them thoroughly and puree in a food processor with 2 teaspoons of salt until smooth. Transfer puree to a large mixing bowl. Add the grated carrot, cumin, breadcrumbs, olive oil, and herbs. Mix well and cool completely. Lightly toast the sesame seeds in a dry skillet until dry and crispy but still light in color. Cool.

With a teaspoon, scoop out portions of the chickpea mixture and form into equal-sized balls until you have used all of the mixture. Spread the sesame seeds out onto a plate and roll each of the croquettes in the seeds to coat.

COD WITH PINE NUTS

Ingredients:

- 2 lbs (1 kg) cod fillet
- 1 ½ cups (250 g) slivered almonds
- 1 lemon
- 1 cup (¼ l) olive oil (*not* extra virgin)
- Cracked black pepper
- salt

Method:

Place the cod onto a cooling rack, then onto a baking tray. Season with salt, lemon, and black pepper. Cover the fillet with an even layer of almonds.

Heat the oil in a skillet just until the oil begins to give off wisps of smoke, then turn off the heat.

Very carefully, spoon the hot oil over the fish, basting repeatedly until you have used all of the oil.

Pour off the excess oil from the baking tray and bake at 300°F for about 8 to 10 minutes. Garnish with more lemon juice, almonds, and pepper.

LAMB STEW

Ingredients:

- 2 lbs (1 kg) lamb meat cut in big dices
- 2 onions
- 6 tablespoons (100 ml) olive oil
- ⅓ cup (40 g) gluten-free flour or cornstarch
- 2 cups (½ l) white wine
- ½ cup vinegar
- 1 cup Brandy
- 3 egg yolks
- 1 lemon
- ½ teaspoon grated nutmeg
- ½ teaspoon rosemary and thyme
- salt and pepper
- butter

Method:

Salt and pepper the lamb meat and dredge in flour to coat evenly. In a large ovenproof Dutch oven on medium heat, sear the meat in oil until browned on all sides. Remove the meat from the Dutch oven and set aside. In the same Dutch oven, sauté the onions in butter until soft. Season with the rosemary, thyme, and grated nutmeg. Return the meat to the Dutch oven. Add the white wine, brandy, and vinegar. Cover and bake until the meat is fork-tender, about 2 hours.

In a small bowl, whisk the egg yolks together. With a ladle, slowly add a little of the hot cooking liquid to the egg yolk while whisking. Continue to add liquid until the mixture is hot, but not scrambled. Stir the egg yolk mixture into the stew to thicken. Season with lemon juice, salt, and pepper to taste.

CHICKEN EMPANADAS

Ingredients:

- 1 recipe of dough for stuffed pastries (pg. 68)
- 3 tablespoons olive oil
- 1 egg
- 1 cup (2 dl) water
- 1 medium onion
- 7 oz (200 g) chicken, finely chopped
- 2 ½ oz (75 g) dry cured ham, chopped
- 1 teaspoon (4 g) fresh thyme, chopped
- 1 teaspoon (4 g) fresh oregano, chopped
- salt

Method:

Peel and chop the onion, then sauté in a tablespoon of olive oil until tender. Add the thyme and oregano to the onions and transfer to a bowl to cool. In the same pan, sear the chicken and ham until brown on all sides. Add the meat to the onions and season to taste. Let stuffing cool completely.

Roll the dough very thin with a rolling pin over a floured table.

Crack the egg into a small bowl and beat until smooth.

With a large cup or pastry ring mold, cut circles out of the dough and put a tablespoon of the filling in the center of each circle. With your finger or a brush, spread a little egg along the rim of the dough. Fold in half and press the edges to seal.

Finally, fry in 375°F oil.

TEMPEH MEDALLIONS GARDEN-STYLE

Ingredients for 2-3 persons:

- 1 piece of tempeh, sliced
- 1 leaf kombu
- 1 tablespoon gluten-free soy sauce

- 2 bay leaves
- 2 carrots
- 1 turnip, finely sliced
- 3 tablespoons corn
- 1 handful green beans cut in half
- ¼ lb. radishes, cut in half
- umeboshi vinegar
- sea salt
- olive oil

Method:

Season all the vegetables (except the radish) with a few pinches of sea salt and steam for 7 to 10 minutes.

Separately, clean then steam the radishes until tender. Season the radishes with umeboshi vinegar to taste.

In a sauce pot, add the tempeh and cover with water. Add the kombu, bay leaves, and gluten-free soy sauce to the water and simmer for 15 minutes. Drain the tempeh carefully.

Pat the tempeh dry with paper towels. Cut the tempeh into slices and griddle on both sides until golden brown. Season with gluten-free soy sauce and keep warm.

Place the steamed veggies on a serving dish, top with the crispy tempeh, and garnish with the radishes.

5. Breads

We chose rice flour as the basic flour for bread-making. This produces a compact crumb with a neutral flavor, which is very well suited to combine with other flavors.

Other gluten-free flours are also good: millet, quinoa, buckwheat, or chestnut. All of them have stronger flavors, but if they are used alone are kind of heavy and produce denser doughs.

Adding buckwheat, millet, or quinoa flakes (as well as sesame, sunflower …) makes breads with different textures and flavors. The fine rice or millet semolinas, and quinoa or amaranth seeds could be added to the rice flour dough for an extra texture and a delightful crumb.

It is easier to use a gluten-free baking powder for these breads (the one used in pastries). It is important to verify the ingredients of the baking powder before using it.

ABOUT GLUTEN-FREE BREAD DOUGHS

Gluten-free bread dough does not require kneading, but it is necessary to get a flexible consistency, which makes the dough rise easily, thanks to the yeast.

The bread dough made with gluten-free flours is soft; therefore it is not possible to work with it like regular bread dough, so it is best to bake it like a cake. For this, choose a round baking pan (cake or tart). To make rolls, scrape the dough into paper cups or tartlet pans.

Do not use a tall baking pan because the bread will be heavy.

Breads made with rice flour don't last long, and it's recommended to eat them the same day that you bake them or the next day. They are so easy to make that you can have fresh baked bread frequently.

QUINOA BREAD WITH RAISINS

Almonds and raisins make this bread the perfect side for salads, raw vegetables, hummus, and more.

Combined with rice flour and buckwheat, the quinoa seeds swell and produce a tender texture. The baking pan must be well greased to get a crispy crust.

Ingredients:
- 1 ½ cups (150 g) rice flour
- ½ cup (50 g) buckwheat flour
- 2 tablespoons (20 g) quinoa seeds
- 1 teaspoon (15 g) baking powder
- 1 teaspoon fine salt
- ¼ cup (50 g) sliced almonds (or walnuts)

- 1 handful Corinto raisins
- 1 cup (25 cl) water
- Olive oil for the pan

Method:

In a bowl add the rice and buckwheat flours, the quinoa seeds, baking powder, salt, almonds, and raisins. Add water and stir vigorously. Pour the mixture in a greased baking pan; the dough is very soft and will look like cake batter.

Bake at 375°F for 25 to 30 minutes. After 15 minutes you may brush the top of the bread with a little olive oil to give a slightly brown color. Unmold and cool on a rack.

This bread is delicious when it is still warm from the oven.

SUNFLOWER AND AMARANTH BREAD TART

In just 30 minutes you can make this bread and have it ready. Bake it before the meal and have it warm from the oven, for a crispy texture from amaranth, and the golden crust, thanks to the olive oil.

Ingredients:

- 2 cups (200 g) rice flour
- 2 tablespoons (20 g) amaranth
- 2 tablespoons (10 g) baking powder
- 1 teaspoon salt
- 1 cup (20 cl) water
- 2 tablespoons (20 g) sunflower seeds
- Olive oil

Method:

In a bowl put the rice flour, baking powder, salt, amaranth, and sunflower seeds. Mix and add water. Stir the batter quickly and pour in a greased baking pan (or a tart pan). The batter is soft and makes a round 10-inch cake.

Bake at 350°F for 25 minutes. The crust is light, but to add color brush it with olive oil after 15 minutes of the baking time.

You can unmold and put the bread upside down in the same baking pan.

THREE SEED AND MILLET SEMOLINA BREAD

Ingredients:

- 2 cups (200 g) rice flour
- 1 cup (100 g) millet semolina
- 3 ¼ teaspoons (18 g) baking powder
- 1 teaspoon salt
- 1 cup (25 cl) water
- 4 tablespoons (40 g) sunflower seeds
- 2 tablespoons sesame seeds
- 1 tablespoon poppy seeds
- Olive oil for the baking pan

Method:

In a bowl, add the rice flour, millet semolina, baking powder, and salt. Add water and combine well.

Stir quickly. It will be very thick.

Sprinkle the seeds in the bottom of a greased 10-inch baking pan (or tart pan). The dough will spread in the pan like a cake batter.

Bake at 375°F for 25 minutes. Unmold, and turn upside down in the same baking pan, showing the seed layer.

CHESTNUT AND HAZELNUT ROLLS

These rolls have a mild flavor thanks to the chestnut flour, which sweetens the dough. They are delicious when warm from the oven.

Ingredients for 6 rolls:

- 2 cups (200 g) rice flour

- ⅔ cup (60 g) chestnut flour
- 1 teaspoon salt
- 2 ¼ teaspoons (12 g) baking powder
- 1 cup (20 cl) water

Optional. 6 tablespoons chopped hazelnuts

Method:

Combine the flours, salt, and baking powder in a bowl. Add water and stir quickly; the dough is foamy and thick.

With your wet hands, and a spatula, work the dough without kneading, and make small balls, the size of tangerines. (For hazelnut rolls, put chopped hazelnuts on top of the dough, pressing them to stick to the dough.)

As soon as the rolls are made, place them on a baking tray lined with parchment paper. Bake in a medium-heat oven for 20 minutes. The surface of the rolls will crack when baking. To obtain a light golden color, brush the rolls after 15 minutes with olive oil. Put back in the oven and bake 5 minutes longer.

QUINOA AND TURMERIC BREAD

A good proportion of quinoa will give a nice crumb to this bread, with a light yellow color thanks to the turmeric. This is perfect to serve with raw salad or sautéed vegetables.

Ingredients:

- 1 cup (100 g) rice flour
- ⅓ cup (60 g) quinoa seeds
- 1 teaspoon (5 g) baking powder
- 2 pinches ground turmeric
- 1 cup (20 cl) water
- ½ teaspoon salt

Method:

Put quinoa, rice flour, baking powder, salt, and turmeric in a bowl; stir, adding water. Then grease a baking pan with oil and pour the batter, which has a loose consistency. The baking pan should be halfway full to make a proper loaf.

Bake at 375°F for 25 minutes. Unmold while hot and cool (so the quinoa seeds finish absorbing the bread's moisture) before serving it.

STEAMED BREAD

You can make rolls without an oven. For this steamed recipe use the dough for sunflower bread.

Ingredients:

- 1 cup (100 g) rice flour
- 1 tablespoon (10 g) amaranth
- 1 teaspoon (5 g) baking powder
- ½ teaspoon salt
- ½ cup (10 cl) water
- 1 tablespoon (10 g) sunflower seeds

Method:

Make the dough as in the sunflower and amaranth bread tart. Pour in ramekins or small baking pans greased with olive oil. The pans must be half full because this dough rises a lot.

Put in a heavy-bottomed saucepan and steam over very low heat for 20 to 25 minutes.

Unmold while warm or serve in the pans.

OLIVE LOAF

Lots of olives and a "milk bread" type of dough, thanks to the combination of rice semolina and rice flour, make an original and flavorful bread.

Ingredients:

- 1 ½ cups (120 g) fine rice semolina
- 1 cup (100 g) rice flour

- 1 teaspoon (5 g) baking powder
- 1 teaspoon salt
- ½ cup + 1 tablespoon (60 ml) olive oil
- ½ cup (120 ml) water
- ¾ cup (120 g) pitted black olives
- 1 pinch thyme or rosemary

Method:

In a bowl put the rice flour and semolina, baking powder, and salt. Stir and add the oil and water at once. Stir in the black olives and thyme; knead lightly with a spatula. Grease a baking pan with oil and pour the dough. With slightly wet hands, stretch the dough to fit the pan.

Bake at 425°F for 25 minutes. After 15 minutes brush the bread with olive oil and finish baking.

Variation: To make a sesame loaf, add 20 g sesame seeds and use half the olives.

6. Rolls

As in bread-making, rice flour is one of the favorites used to make rolls. Millet or rice semolina can be incorporated to give the dough a better texture.

Incorporate orange flower water to add an aroma to the dough, because it is delicately fragrant and goes well with the other ingredients of the rolls and with the toppings.

Cut in slices; the rolls with orange flower water fragrance can be spread with fruit marmalades, honey, etc.

If we want to scent the milk rolls with an essential oil, choose an organic one, with a citrus aroma. Try to use it in small amounts, about three or six drops of bergamot, lemon, or grapefruit oil, which will give it a lovely fragrance.

Orange or lemon zest is a good ingredient to add to the dough. A milk roll is perfect with aniseed or a pinch of ground cinnamon.

Non-hydrogenated vegetable margarine is the best fat to use in these rolls, because it is easy to beat with sugar, making a cream that acts as the base for other ingredients. On the other hand, olive oil works well for a dough made with fine semolina (rice or millet). It's interesting to note that the characteristic olive oil aroma is not obvious after the bread has been baked. It's very mild. If you like this alternative you can make a vanilla-infused olive oil at home. Put a scraped vanilla bean in an olive oil bottle, and wait a few weeks before using it. A quicker option is to scrape the vanilla seeds from a vanilla bean and stir into a bottle of olive oil, or add a pinch of vanilla powder.

If you sweeten the dough with raw brown sugar, it will render its aroma, and this will be enough. If you choose an essential oil or orange flower water, make sure that you use a light raw brown sugar in the recipe, with a milder flavor. On the other hand, if you want to go sugar-free, fruits (raisins, for instance) could give enough sweetness to the dough. A sweeter option is to add choco-late chips to the dough. For a "panettone" style dough, add can-died fruit or just raisins and finely chopped candied orange peel.

ROLL WITH GRAPES

This dough is made with rice flour, and has a crumbly texture that melts in the mouth. It is scented with orange flower water, perfect for breakfast. Because it is not very sweet, you can have it as toast with honey or marmalade.

Ingredients:

- ¾ cup (160 g) vegetable margarine, at room temperature
- ⅔ cup (146 g) raw brown sugar
- 2 eggs
- 2 ¼ cups (240 g) rice flour

- 2 teaspoons (10 g) baking powder
- 10 tablespoons rice milk
- 6 tablespoons orange flower water
- ⅓ cup (50 g) raisins

Method:

Beat with sugar until creamy and add the eggs, one by one, beating well after each addition.

Add half the rice flour, baking powder, rice milk, and orange flower water. Finally, add the remaining rice flour.

Stir in the raisins and pour the batter into a round baking pan (or in small round pans), and bake at 375°F for 20 minutes. Turn the heat to 400°F and continue baking for 15 minutes.

CAKE WITH LEMON ZEST AND SEMOLINA

In this cake, millet semolina is combined with rice flour. This semolina is extremely fine and gives the batter a light texture. The cake is not particularly sweet and has a fluffy texture, perfect for breakfast and as a snack.

Ingredients:

- ¼ cup (60 ml) olive oil
- ¼ cup (50 g) millet semolina
- 3 eggs
- 2 tablespoons (14 g) raw brown sugar
- ⅔ cup (80 g) rice flour
- 1 teaspoon (5 g) baking powder
- 1 lemon

Method:

Put the olive oil in a bowl and combine with the semolina. Add the eggs, one by one, and then the rice flour, sugar, and baking powder. Grate the lemon and add the zest to the mixture. Pour the batter into a greased baking pan. Bake in the oven heated to 400°F for 35 minutes. Unmold and cool.

CAKE WITH FRUITS

This is made with fine rice semolina. The essential oil gives a very mild fragrance to the cake, and the final texture is tender and easy to slice. It does not have any sugar in it but the fruits give enough sweetness to make it delicately sweet. Serve it with marmalade.

Ingredients:

- ¼ cup (60 ml) mild olive oil
- ¼ cup (50 g) rice semolina
- 3 eggs
- ⅔ cup (80 g) rice flour
- 1 teaspoon (5 g) baking powder
- 1 pear, thinly sliced
- 6 drops grapefruit essential oil

Variation: Substitute the pear and the essential oil with 1 banana and a pinch of ground cinnamon.

Method:

Put the olive oil in a bowl and combine with the semolina flour and the eggs. Add the rice flour and baking powder. Stir in the essential oil and the sliced pear (or the sliced banana and ground cinnamon).

Pour into a greased loaf pan. Bake at 375°F for 35 minutes. Unmold and cool.

7. Pastries and Tarts

Rice flour is a wonderful ingredient to make all kinds of pies. It can be used on its own, but combined with other ingredients like almond flour, for example, or fine rice semolina, you can get different and delicious textures.

Quinoa and chestnut flour, which have stronger flavors, are better used as a complement to the rice flour. You can add them in small quantities or combine with other ingredients like hazelnut puree or cacao.

Chestnut flour goes well with hazelnut and almond flour or paste, chocolate, apple, pear and others.

To make sure the dough will bake properly it is best to make the pies thin and use cake or tart pans. This way the gluten-free dough will have a tender and moist texture, and will cook quickly.

Although the cooking is slightly more delicate, these recipes are good to bake in a loaf pan, perfect to cut in thick slices. The only thing you need to do is to bake the pies in a moderate oven, give the batter the chance to grow, and cook evenly.

Some pastries don't need any fats. Other recipes will benefit when almond or hazelnut paste, which are amazing vegetable "butters," are added to the preparation, rendering their tempting aroma to cakes and biscuits. Generally speaking, these ingredients produce pastries with a dominant nut flavor profile.

Use organic margarines instead of hydrogenated ones for best flavor.

ALMOND CAKE WITH ORANGE ZEST

Ingredients:

- ⅓ cup (80 g) margarine
- ½ cup (110 g) raw brown sugar
- ½ cup (50 g) ground almonds
- 3 eggs
- 1 ¼ cups (120 g) rice flour
- 1 teaspoon (5 g) baking powder
- 6 drops vanilla essence
- 1 orange

Method:

Melt the margarine over low heat. Turn off the heat and combine with sugar, ground almonds, and vanilla essence. Add the eggs, one by one. Stir in the rice flour and baking powder. Grate the orange and add one tablespoon of zest to the mixture.

Pour the batter into a greased loaf pan. Bake 10 minutes at 375°F. Turn the oven a little higher and continue baking for 15 to 20 minutes. This cake will turn golden brown in a few minutes, so you will need to protect it during the baking time.

CHOCOLATE IMPERIAL

This is a creamy cake to have warm as dessert, with an almond sauce, crème anglaise (custard), or Seville orange marmalade. Choose a dark chocolate with a minimum of 60 percent cacao.

Ingredients:

- 1 cup + 2 tablespoons (200 g) dark chocolate for baking
- ½ cup (100 g) vegetable margarine
- ⅓ cup (74 g) raw brown sugar
- ¼ cup (20 g) quinoa flour
- 4 eggs

Method:

Melt chocolate and margarine in a saucepan over low heat. Turn off the heat, and add the sugar and quinoa flour to the chocolate mixture. Add egg yolks, one by one. Whip the egg whites to soft peaks and gently fold in to the chocolate mixture. Pour the batter into a greased cake pan and bake in the oven, 400 to 425°F, for 25 minutes. Serve with pastry cream.

CINNAMON SWIRL

The fragrance of this lovely cake is delicious. Serve it with fruit salad or fruit compote. If you love cinnamon you may double the amount given in this recipe. Good for breakfast or tea time.

Ingredients:

- ⅓ cup (80 g) vegetable margarine, at room temp
- 1 ¼ cups (275 g) raw brown sugar
- ⅓ cup (30 g) almond flour
- 3 eggs
- 1 ¼ cups (120 g) rice flour
- 1 teaspoon (5g) baking powder
- 1 tablespoon ground cinnamon

Method:

Mix with the sugar and almond flour. Add the eggs, one by one. Add the rice flour and baking powder. Combine and pour half the batter into a greased baking pan. Add the cinnamon to the remaining batter and put in the pan, swirling as you mix the batter with a spatula. Bake 25 to 30 minutes at 375°F. The cake is ready when you pierce it with the tip of a knife and it comes clean and dry.

PEAR TART WITH HAZELNUT PASTE

Ingredients:

- ¼ cup + 1 tablespoon (70 g) hazelnut paste, at room temp
- ¾ cup (187 g) raw sugar
- 3 eggs
- ⅓ cup (30 g) rice flour
- 1 tablespoon baking powder
- 2 pears, thinly sliced
- 3 or 4 tablespoons chopped hazelnuts

Method:

Use a smooth hazelnut paste at room temperature. If the oil and the paste are separated you must shake it or mix it with a fork until smooth.

Put paste in a bowl and combine with the egg yolks. Add sugar. In a separate bowl, whip the egg whites until soft peaks and pour half in the bowl with the hazelnut mixture. Fold and add the rice flour and baking powder. Finally fold in the remaining egg whites.

Peel and thinly slice the pears. Grease a baking pan with a bit of oil, scrape the batter into the pan, and arrange the pear slices on top. They will sink in the batter.

Bake approximately 30 minutes at 375°F. Unmold and garnish with chopped hazelnuts.

APPLE TART

Ingredients:
- ½ cup (100 g) vegetable margarine, at room temp
- ½ cup (120 g) pear or apple concentrate (or pear syrup)
- 1 cup (100 g) rice flour
- 3 eggs
- 2 apples, peeled and sliced
- ground cinnamon

Method:

Bring the margarine to room temperature. Combine with the fruit concentrate. Add one egg and rice flour, mix well, and add the remaining eggs.

Peel and slice the apples. Scrape the batter into an oiled tart baking pan and place the apple in concentric circles.

Bake at 375°F for 30 minutes. Dust with cinnamon.

PISTACHIO CAKE WITH CHOCOLATE CHIPS

In the center of this delicious cake you'll find pear chunks, pistachios, and chocolate. You can bake the cake in paper cups for a nice presentation or to eat as a snack.

Ingredients:
- ½ cup (100 g) vegetable margarine
- 1 ¼ cups (275 g) raw brown sugar (+ 2 tablespoons to garnish)
- 1 cup (100 g) rice flour

- 3 eggs
- 1 pear (or 1 apple), peeled and chopped
- 20 pistachios, peeled and unsalted (+ more for garnishing)
- 20 chocolate chips

Method:

Melt the margarine in a small saucepan over low heat. Turn off the heat. Add the sugar and combine. Add rice flour and eggs, stirring well.

Peel and chop the pear. Combine the batter with the pear, chocolate chips, and pistachios. Pour into a greased loaf pan (or paper cups) and bake at 375°F for 25 to 35 minutes.

Chop the remaining pistachios, combine with the remaining sugar, and sprinkle over the cooled cake.

CAKE WITH ORANGE CARAMEL

Ingredients:

- ½ cup (100 g) vegetable margarine, room temp
- 1 ¼ cups (275 g) raw brown sugar
- 3 eggs
- 1 cup (100 g) rice flour
- 4 drops tangerine essence
- 1 orange, peeled and thinly sliced
- 3 tablespoons raw brown sugar for the bottom of the pan

Method:

Bring the margarine to room temperature. Beat with the sugar; add one egg, the rice flour, and the remaining eggs. Mix vigorously and add the tangerine essence.

Grease the bottom of a baking pan with margarine. Layer the bottom of the pan with the orange slices and sprinkle with 3 tablespoons sugar, and then cover with the batter. Bake for 20 minutes at 375°F. Unmold while still warm, before the caramel sticks to the bottom of the pan.

GRAND CACAO DESSERT

Ingredients:

- ⅔ cup (100 g) dark chocolate (70 percent cacao)
- ¾ cup (150 g) vegetable margarine
- 1 ¼ cups (275 g) raw brown sugar
- 4 eggs
- 6 oz (200 g) cooked chestnuts (buy them already cooked in vacuum-sealed bags)
- A handful of almonds, sliced lengthwise
- 1 teaspoon vanilla essence
- Unsweetened cacao powder

Method:

This is a flourless cake with a lovely texture. Rich in chocolate, it has bits of chestnuts.

Melt the chocolate with the margarine and sugar, over low heat. Turn off the heat, cool a little bit, and add the egg yolks, one by one, whisking vigorously. Add vanilla essence.

Add the chestnuts and stir with a wooden spoon.

In a separate bowl, beat the egg whites until firm, and fold into the chocolate mixture. Pour into a baking pan and bake for 25 minutes at 375°F. Cool before serving the cake but do not refrigerate because it should have a soft texture.

CAKE WITH LEMON SYRUP

This lovely dessert almost melts in your mouth. The batter is made with potato starch, and absorbs the lemon syrup very well. If the lemons are too acidic, reduce the amount of lemon juice and dilute with water or with more agave nectar.

Ingredients:

- 1 cup + 2 tablespoons (160 g) raw brown sugar
- ½ cup (50 g) potato starch
- ½ cup (50 g) rice flour

- 3 ¼ teaspoons (18 g) baking powder
- 3 eggs
- 2 tablespoons olive oil

Lemon syrup:

- 3 lemons
- ½ cup (10 cl) agave nectar

Method:

Combine the rice flour, potato starch, raw brown sugar, and baking powder in a bowl. Add eggs and olive oil, stirring briskly.

Using a vegetable peeler, peel three thin pieces of lemon peel and with a paring knife cut thin strips, like matchsticks. Add to the batter, which should be somewhat foamy.

Pour the batter into a greased baking pan. Bake at 375°F for 20 to 30 minutes, checking every now and then to make sure the cake will not turn dark brown, because this batter bakes quickly.

To make the lemon syrup:

Squeeze the lemons (to obtain about ¾ cup (20 cl) of juice) and pour in a small saucepan. Turn the heat to low and add the agave nectar.

Take the cake out of the oven and pour the hot syrup on top of the hot cake. Cool.

GINGER AND CACAO BAKE

This is a light cake made with dark chocolate and enhanced with a pinch of ginger and pear slices.

Ingredients:

- ⅔ cup (100 g) dark chocolate (70 percent cacao)
- 6 tablespoons (40 g) rice flour
- 4 eggs
- 2 pears, peeled and thinly sliced
- 8 tablespoons vegetable milk (rice or soy)

- 4 tablespoons mild olive oil
- A thin ginger slice
- 2-3 tablespoons brown sugar for a sweeter cake (optional)

Method:

In a small saucepan heat chocolate with vegetable milk over medium-heat until the chocolate melts. Add olive oil. Mix well and cool to room temperature. Add egg yolks, one by one, and then the flour, stirring until smooth. Finely chop the ginger slice or pass through a garlic press. Add to the batter.

In a separate bowl, beat the egg whites until firm and fold into the batter. Pour into a greased baking pan, or you may want to line the pan with parchment paper. Peel and slice the pears, and put on top of the batter. Bake at 375°F. Do not unmold; cut the cake in the pan. If you want to unmold it, you should line the pan with parchment paper before baking.

AMARANTH SNOW CAKE

Ingredients:

- 1 cup (100 g) chestnut flour
- ⅓ cup (80 g) hazelnut paste, at room temp
- 1 ¼ cups (100 g) sugar
- 3 eggs
- ½ cup (10 cl) rice milk
- 1 teaspoon (5 g) baking powder
- 2 tablespoons (20 g) ground cacao
- 1-2 handfuls puffed amaranth (20-30 g)

Frosting:

- 1 ⅓ cups (200 g) dark chocolate (70 percent cacao)
- 5 tablespoons rice milk (or water)
- 1 cup (250 ml) soy cream (it should be liquid)

■ Vanilla bean paste or 4 drops orange essential oil (optional)
Method:
In a bowl combine egg yolks with hazelnut paste (at room temperature, must be fluid and smooth) and add sugar. Stir this mixture and add rice milk, chestnut flour, cacao, and baking powder. Beat the egg whites until firm and fold into the batter.

Pour in a baking pan and bake for 20 minutes at medium-high heat.

To make frosting, melt the chocolate with rice milk or water, add the soy cream, a few tablespoons at a time, stirring constantly over very low heat, and putting the saucepan on and off the burner. The sauce should be creamy and warm. Add the optional vanilla or orange essential oil, and spread on top of the cake with a spatula or the back of a spoon.

Sprinkle the puffed amaranth on top of the frosting and cool.

APPLE-CREAM TART

This dough is a shortcut pastry (made with flour, sugar and egg, so tender that it melts in the mouth), thanks to the combination of rice flour and almond flour. Under the fruit layer, the soy cream makes a creamy filling seasoned with cinnamon.

Ingredients:
■ ⅓ cup (60 g) margarine, at room temp
■ ⅔ cup (146 g) raw brown sugar
■ ⅔ cup (60 g) almond flour
■ 2 eggs
■ 2 ½ cups (250 g) rice flour
Filling:
■ ½ cup (120 g) thick soy cream

- 2 tablespoons raw brown sugar
- Pinch ground cinnamon
- 1 tablespoon almond flour
- 1 tablespoon candied orange peel
- 1 tablespoon raisins
- 3-4 apples

Method:

Beat margarine, at room temperature, with sugar, almond flour, and eggs. Add enough of the rice flour to make a dough that can be formed into a ball. To roll the dough easily, cover with a plastic film and roll on a piece of parchment. Transfer to a tart pan.

To make the filling combine the soy cream with the sugar, cinnamon, almond flour, and dried fruits. Pour in the tart pan on top of the dough. Place the apple slices on top, overlapping to make a pretty design. Bake for 30 to 40 minutes at medium-heat.

STRAWBERRY TART OVER ALMOND CAKE

A cake batter baked in a large tart pan makes the base for this lovely dessert. Cover with the pastry cream (or a vanilla pastry cream made with soy or rice) before topping with the strawberries. The same dessert goes extremely well with raspberries.

Ingredients:

- 8 to 10 oz (250 to 300 g) strawberries
- ⅓ cup (80 g) vegetable margarine, at room temperature
- 1 ¼ cups (275 g) raw brown sugar
- ⅓ cup (30 g) almond flour
- 3 eggs
- 1 ¼ cups (120 g) rice flour
- 1 teaspoon (5 g) baking powder

Pastry cream:
- 2 egg yolks
- ½ cup (110 g) raw brown sugar
- ⅓ cup (40 g) rice flour
- 1 ½ cups (30 cl) soy milk, rice or almond
- 1 teaspoon rose water (optional)

Method:

Beat the margarine with the sugar, and add the almond flour and the eggs, one by one. Stir in the rice flour and the baking powder. Mix well and pour the batter in a large tart pan lined with parchment paper.

Cut a circle of parchment paper big enough to completely line the crust. Use the 2 cups of dried beans to weigh down the parchment. Bake for 10 minutes in a medium-heat oven then turn the heat to high and bake 15 minutes longer.

In a small saucepan combine egg yolks with the sugar. Add rice flour and vegetable milk. Cook over low heat, stirring constantly until thick. Turn off the heat and add the rose water. Unmold the tart and frost with the warm pastry cream. Cool.

Garnish with whole strawberries, if they are small, or cut in half if large. Serve immediately.

ORANGE TART

This tart has a delicious orange scent that also infuses the shortcrust pastry. This dough is also perfect for making a lemon tart.

Ingredients:

Pastry:
- ⅓ cup (60 g) vegetable margarine
- ½ cup + 1 tablespoon (125 g) raw sugar
- ½ cup + 1 tablespoon (60 g) almond flour
- 2 eggs
- 2 ½ cups (250 g) rice flour
- Peel of 1 orange

Filling:

- 2 oranges
- 2 tablespoons rice cream
- 2 eggs
- 4 tablespoons raw sugar

Method:

Bring the margarine to room temperature. Put in the food processor with the sugar, almond flour, eggs, and rice flour.

Grate the orange. You will need about ½ teaspoon zest. Add to the margarine mixture and process until it forms a ball. Add a little extra flour if needed.

This dough should be very easy to work with, although not easy to roll. Put it in the baking pan and press it, working it into the corners with your fingertips. You may use small tartlet pans. To roll, place the dough on a parchment paper, cover with plastic film, and roll.

Transfer the dough to a baking pan.

To make the filling:

In a bowl put the juice from the oranges and two pieces of the peel. Add the rice cream, eggs, and sugar.

Whip until smooth. Pour on the tart shell and bake for 30 to 35 minutes at 375°F.

CHESTNUT CREAM TART

A thin chestnut dough baked in a tart pan makes a wonderful shell for this delicious filling: a chocolate layer under a chestnut cream layer.

Ingredients:

- ⅓ cup (70 g) almond paste, at room temperature
- ⅞ cup (193 g) raw brown sugar
- 3 eggs
- ½ cup (50 g) chestnut flour
- ½ cup (50 g) dark chocolate (70 percent cacao)

- 1 jar (220 g) chestnut cream (with sugar)
- Chocolate to make chocolate shavings (optional)

Method:

Beat the almond paste with the sugar and eggs. Mix well and add the chestnut flour (sifted to avoid lumps).

Spoon the dough into a tart baking pan (lined with parchment paper) and bake for 20 minutes at 375°F. As soon as it comes out of the oven, sprinkle the chocolate, and when it melts, spread with a spatula. Cool. When the chocolate is firm, pour the chestnut cream and spread to cover the entire chocolate layer. Garnish with chocolate shavings.

NOUGATINE TARTLETS

When plain, this dough makes beautiful cookies.

Ingredients:

- 3 tablespoons (20 g) chestnut flour
- 1 cup (100 g) hazelnuts (+ for garnish)
- ½ cup + 1 tablespoon (70 g) confectioners' sugar
- 3 tablespoons rice milk

Filling:

- ⅔ cup (100 g) dark chocolate
- ½ cup (112 g) soy cream (pureed firm tofu)
- 4 tablespoons rice milk
- 2 tablespoons raw brown sugar
- 2 drops tangerine or orange essential oil
- 1 piece candied orange peel

Method:

Chop the hazelnuts in the food processor. Mix chestnut flour, confectioners' sugar, hazelnut paste, and rice milk. Spoon the dough onto a baking tray lined with parchment paper. Press with the side of a knife until it is about ¾ inch thick. Bake for 20 minutes at 375°F. Take out of the oven, cut in squares, and cool.

In a saucepan over low heat melt the chocolate with rice milk and sugar. Turn off the heat, and add soy cream and tangerine oil. Stir vigorously or beat with a mixer until smooth. Refrigerate at least for an hour until it thickens.

Cut the candied orange peel in very thin slices. Using a teaspoon place small portions of cream on top of each tartlet to make small domes. Garnish some tartlets with hazelnuts, and others with candied orange peel. Arrange them in trays to make a pretty display.

APRICOT TART WITH ALMOND CRUMBLE

This dough is lightly sweetened with rice syrup, and the almond crumble adds to the natural sweetness of the apricots.

Ingredients:

- ¾ cup (70 g) quinoa flour
- 1 ½ cups (160 g) rice flour
- ⅓ cup (80 g) rice syrup or honey
- 3 ½ tablespoons (30 g) olive oil
- a few tablespoons vegetable milk
- 2 apricots

Crumble:

- 1 ½ cups (150 g) almond flour
- 1 ¼ cups (275 g) raw brown sugar
- 1 teaspoon ground cinnamon

Method:

Combine the flours, rice syrup, and olive oil in the bowl of a food processor. Process a few minutes, adding a few tablespoons of vegetable milk to make a smooth dough. Roll the dough on a lightly floured surface.

Seed the apricots and cut each one in four pieces. Place them on top of the dough, cut side up. Bake at 375°F for 15 minutes.

In the meantime combine almond flour with sugar and cinnamon to sprinkle the apricots. Bake for 15 minutes longer until the crumble has a nice golden brown color.

KIWI TARTLETS

A vanilla-flavored cream and coconut make this a festive dessert.

Ingredients for 5-6 tartlets:

- ⅓ cup (80 g) coconut cream at room temperature
- ¾ cup (165 g) raw brown sugar
- 1 ½ cups (150 g) rice flour

For the vanilla cream:

- 6 tablespoons (40 g) rice flour
- 1 cup (25 cl) rice milk
- ½ vanilla bean
- 2 tablespoons raw brown sugar
- 3 or 4 kiwi
- Tropical fruits: mango, pineapple, papaya, banana, etc.

Garnish:

- 3 tablespoons grated coconut

Method:

Mix coconut cream until smooth and creamy. In a bowl combine raw sugar and coconut cream. Add rice flour and stir until thick. It should make a ball. Divide in several portions, put each one in a tartlet pan, and press with your fingertips to make a shell (it's hard to roll it with the rolling pin because it is sticky). Bake for 20 minutes at 375°F.

To make the vanilla cream, dissolve the rice flour in the rice milk. Cook in a saucepan over low heat, stirring constantly until thick. Add the sugar and stir until dissolved. When it's very thick, turn off the heat. Slice the vanilla bean and scrape out the seeds with the tip of a knife, and add to the cream.

Pour the warm vanilla cream on the unmolded and cold pastry shells. Before serving, peel the kiwi (and the other fruits, if using) and layer on top of the cream. Garnish with grated coconut.

8. Crumbles and Puddings

Almond flour, combined with ground cinnamon and sugar, makes for a delicious crumble, quick and easy to create, without any added fat because the almonds are rich in fats. This powder absorbs the fruit juice, has a pretty golden brown color, and is a wonderful dessert. Besides, it can be made with ground hazelnuts, grated coconut, or coconut flour.

To make a crumble it is best to use chestnut flour. Buckwheat is another ingredient suitable for this. It has a distinct flavor, so it is a good idea to combine it with hazelnut flour.

Another idea is to use rice flakes, combined with margarine and sugar, to make a crispier crumble.

Use the sugar of your preference, raw brown sugar or confectioners', or perhaps substitute with rice syrup. You may add raisins, chopped dates, or chopped dried apricots to the crumble, in place of the sugar, if you like your desserts less sweet or if the compote is too sweet.

Puddings are usually made with leftover bread or grated bread. You can substitute cereal flakes to make this dessert lighter and easier to digest. We have opted for rice flakes to which you may add quinoa or millet flakes in small quantities because they have a strong flavor. Eggs can be substituted with bananas, which helps give the pudding a richer texture.

FRUIT PUDDING WITH RICE FLAKES

Coconut milk gives a pleasant and exotic aroma, and if you like the flavor, you can substitute up to $\frac{1}{3}$ of the rice milk.

Dried pineapple can be substituted with dried apricots, dried mangoes, candied fruit, or prunes.

Ingredients:

- 1 ½ cups (150 g) rice flakes
- 1 ½ cups (30 cl) rice milk
- 4 tablespoons coconut milk
- 4 tablespoons dried pineapple
- 1 handful raisins
- ⅜ cup (83 g) raw brown sugar
- 2 eggs
- 2 bananas (or 1 apple and 1 banana)

Method:

Place the flakes in a bowl and soak in the rice milk and coconut milk for 15 minutes. Add the chopped dried fruit (pineapple, mango, apricot, or raisins). Add sugar and mix with the eggs.

Cut the fresh fruit in slices and combine with the milk mixture. Pour in a greased loaf pan and bake at 375°F for 30 to 40 minutes (depending on the baking pan used and the thickness of the pudding).

CHESTNUT PUDDING

It takes only 10 minutes to make and it's a tasty dessert for chestnut cream lovers. It melts in the mouth and goes perfectly well with chocolate chips (that help to sweeten the pudding), with a handful of raisins or with 5 or 6 seeded and chopped prunes.

Ingredients:

- 1 (400 g) jar chestnut puree
- 2 eggs
- ⅔ cup (146 g) raw brown sugar
- ⅓ cup (50 g) chocolate chips
- ½ cup (50 g) quinoa flour
- 1 teaspoon baking powder

Method:

In a bowl mix the chestnut puree with the eggs. Add sugar, quinoa flour, baking powder, and chocolate chips.

Pour in a greased baking pan and bake for 25 minutes in at 375°F.

Unmold or cut directly in the baking pan.

PLUM CRUMBLE WITH CRISPY RICE

This is a great dessert to have warm or cold, to enjoy the fragrant texture of the plums with the crispy rice flakes. It's also delicious if you use fresh figs in place of the plums.

Ingredients:

- 1 ¼ cups (275 g) raw brown sugar
- 1 cup (100 g) vegetable margarine, at room temp
- 1 ½ cups (150 g) toasted rice flakes
- ¾ cup (50 g) chopped dried apple
- 3 tablespoons sesame seeds
- 12 plums

Method:

Chop the plums and place in the bottom of a greased baking tray. Beat the margarine, at room temperature, with the sugar, the flakes, sesame seeds, and dried apple, and sprinkle on top of the plums. Bake for 25 minutes at 375°F.

BANANA PUDDING WITH CINNAMON SAUCE

This is an eggless pudding with rice flakes. Bananas bind the mixture, producing a lovely dessert that goes well with custard or fruit cream.

Ingredients:

- 2 bananas
- 1 ¼ cups (120 g) rice flakes
- 3 ½ cups (850 g) soy milk

- ¾ cup (165 g) raw brown sugar
- 1 handful raisins

For the cinnamon sauce:
- 1 tablespoon (20 g) rice cream
- 2 tablespoons (30 g) vanilla flavored soy milk
- 3 tablespoons agave syrup
- ½ teaspoon ground cinnamon

Method:

In a bowl combine the rice flakes and soy milk. In the meantime, mash bananas with a fork. Add this puree to the flakes along with sugar and raisins. Pour in a greased loaf pan.

Bake for 30-35 minutes at 375°F. Cool for several minutes if you want to unmold, or cut directly in the pan.

To make the cinnamon sauce:

Dissolve the rice cream with cinnamon and soy milk (if you use regular milk, add a bit of sugar). Cook over low heat until thick, stirring continuously. The cream should be thick enough to cover the back of a spoon, but at the same time continue to drip.

Turn off the heat, sweeten the sauce to your liking (with agave syrup), and cool in a saucer. It will thicken as it cools.

Turn off the heat, sweeten the sauce to your liking, and cool in a saucer. It will thicken as it cools.

MILLET GRATIN WITH MARMALADE

Ingredients:
- 1 cup (120 g) fine millet semolina
- 2 cups (45 cl) almond milk (rice or soy)
- 3 to 5 tablespoons orange marmalade (cherry or apricot)
- 2 eggs
- 2 apples, peeled and thinly sliced

Method:

Dissolve the millet semolina with the vegetable milk and heat gently. When it comes to a boil add the marmalade, stirring constantly because the mixture will thicken. It's ready in one minute. Turn off the heat, add apples, peeled and thinly sliced. When the mixture is somewhat cold, stir in the eggs, one by one. Do not add the egg when the mixture is hot because the eggs will curdle.

Grease a small gratin pan or several small ones, pour the mixture, and bake in a medium-heat oven for 25 minutes. Serve warm or cold.

COCONUT CRUMBLE

This delicious dessert combines with a rhubarb marmalade made with bananas and sweetened with raisins, with a coconut crumble. Remember that rhubarb can be cut in pieces and macerated in sugar to tame its acidity.

Ingredients:

- 6-8 rhubarb ribs
- 2 bananas
- ½ cup (50 g) margarine, at room temp
- 3 tablespoons (20 g) rice flour
- ½ cup (110 g) raw brown sugar
- 1 handful raisins
- Grated coconut
- Rice syrup or cane sugar (optional)

Method:

Clean the rhubarb ribs, take out the fiber, and chop. Add the sliced bananas and rhubarb to a heavy-bottom sauce pot and cook over very low heat, for 15 minutes.

In the meantime mix the margarine at room temperature with sugar and rice flour. Add enough grated coconut to make a crumbly mixture.

Add raisins to the rhubarb-banana compote (if it's too acidic, add some sugar or rice syrup) and pour on a greased baking tray. Cover with the coconut mixture.

Broil for 10-15 minutes until the crumble melts and turns golden brown. Serve cold or warm.

TUTTI FRUTTI CRUMBLE

An easy crumble made with a mixture of almond flour, sugar, and cinnamon.

Ingredients:
- 6 peaches
- plums
- 1 ½ cups (150 g) almond flour
- 1 ¼ cups (312 g) raw brown sugar
- 1 teaspoon ground cinnamon

Method:
Make a fruit compote with the chopped peaches and plums, cooked over very low heat. The fruit should keep its shape.

Meanwhile combine almond flour, sugar, and cinnamon. Pour the compote in a greased baking tray. Sprinkle with the almond flour mixture. Bake for 15 minutes at 375°F, until the crumble is golden brown.

APPLE CRUMBLE WITH CHESTNUT FLOUR

The combination of chestnut flour and ground cinnamon complements the fruit with its spicy fragrance.

Ingredients:
- 1 ½ cups (150 g) chestnut flour
- 1 ½ cups (330 g) raw brown sugar
- ¾ cup (80 g) vegetable margarine
- 1 teaspoon ground cinnamon
- 8 apples
- Juice of ½ lemon

Method:

Peel the apples and chop them. Add the lemon juice and cook over low heat to make a compote.

Mix the margarine with sugar, flour, and cinnamon, until crumbly or process in a food processor until it looks like oatmeal.

Pour the compote on a greased baking tray, and top with the crumble, pressing well to make a firm layer. Bake in a hot oven for 10 to 15 minutes.

CHOCOLATE AND HAZELNUT GRATIN

To make this gratin, the chestnut flakes must be soaked the day before. Bake in a large baking tray or in several round earthenware cups used for Catalan Cream (or crème brûlee).

Ingredients:

- 1 ½ cups (150 g) toasted chestnut flakes
- 2 cups rice milk
- ⅓ cup (50 g) dark chocolate
- ⅔ cup (70 g) hazelnut flour

Method:

Pour the rice milk over the chestnut flakes and soak overnight.

In a saucepan over low heat, put the chopped chocolate and the chestnut flakes mixture. When the chocolate melts, turn off the heat and add the hazelnut flour. You may use store-bought ground hazelnuts or make your own in the food processor, giving a crunchier texture.

This batter is very liquidy, and the chestnut flakes absorb the chocolate milk in the oven. Pour on a greased baking tray and bake at 375°F for 15 to 20 minutes (keep an eye on it to avoid overcooking). Cool completely before serving.

BANANA GRATIN WITH CARDAMOM

This dessert is very easy to make, and it looks beautiful if served in ramekins.

Ingredients:

- 4 bananas
- 4 tablespoons rice flour
- 6 tablespoons coconut cream
- 4 tablespoons maple syrup
- ¾ cup (15 cl) rice milk
- ½ teaspoon ground cardamom
- 3 tablespoons almond flour

Method:

Mix the rice flour, coconut cream, and rice milk in a small saucepan. Cook over low heat, stirring constantly until thickened. It looks like a pastry cream. Sweeten with maple syrup.

Peel the bananas and mash with a fork. Mix with the cream and pour onto a greased baking tray.

Dust with almond flour and ground cardamom. Broil less than 10 minutes. Cool before serving.

9. Cookies and Sweet Bites

MATCHA TEA AND PISTACHIO BITES

Matcha is a Japanese green tea that comes in powder form (it is originally from Thailand). Used in pastries it gives a bright green color and the delicate flavor of green tea.

Ingredients:

- ⅔ cup (30 g) vegetable margarine
- 1 ¼ cups (275 g) raw brown sugar
- 4 eggs
- 1 ⅓ cups (130 g) rice flour
- 1 teaspoon (5 g) baking powder

- 2 tablespoons matcha tea
- 1 cup (100 g) unsalted and peeled pistachios

Melt the margarine in a saucepan over low heat. Add sugar and stir. Then add rice flour, baking powder, and green tea. Incorporate the eggs, one by one, and combine well.

Pour the batter in small baking pans, greased. Sprinkle with pistachios. Bake at medium-high heat for 10 to 15 minutes, depending on the size of the baking pans. Unmold when still hot.

COCONUT ROCKS

Rice syrup gives a light sweetness, and the rice cream helps to bind the mixture. Buy rice cream in small bags. It looks like precooked flour.

Ingredients for 10-12 rocks:

- 1 cup (120 g) grated coconut
- ½ cup (140 g) rice syrup
- 2 tablespoons (40 g) rice cream

Method:

Stir coconut and rice syrup, and add the rice cream. Combine well. Place a dozen mounds on a greased baking tray.

Bake at 350°F for 10 to 15 minutes. The darker the color they get in the oven, the crispier they will be. If you want them chewy in the center, don't let them turn too golden brown.

Unmold carefully with a spatula and cool before serving.

DATE COOKIES

These cookies, sweetened with rice syrup and dates, get a chewy texture when cooking and are great as snacks or to take to picnics.

Ingredients for 10 cookies:

- 1 cup rice flour
- 1 cup buckwheat flour
- 1 tablespoon baking powder

- 5 tablespoons chopped almonds
- ½ cup mild olive oil
- ½ cup rice milk
- 5 tablespoons rice syrup
- 10 dates

Method:

Coarsely chop the almonds in a food processor. Combine with the flours and baking powder. Add olive oil, rice milk, and rice syrup.

Discard the dates' seeds and chop them. Add them to the batter, which should be very thick. Using a spoon and a spatula place mounds, the size of walnuts, on a baking tray lined with parchment paper. Press each one lightly with the back of a spoon. Bake at 375°F for 25 minutes or until golden brown.

Variation: Use honey instead of rice syrup.

COCONUT LITTLE DEVILS

These bites, very chewy and semi-covered with a chocolate glaze, are delicious for kids and adults alike. They are perfect to have as a snack.

Ingredients for 12 bites:

- 2 cups (440 g) raw brown sugar
- ⅔ cup (100 g) grated coconut
- ½ cup (50 g) rice flour
- 2 egg whites
- 1 teaspoon baking powder
- ⅔ cup (100 g) dark chocolate
- 5 or 6 tablespoons rice milk

Method:

In a bowl combine sugar and coconut, and stir in the egg whites. Add flour and baking powder. Pour the batter in small muffin baking pans that are greased or lined with paper cups.

Bake for 10 minutes at 375°F. Turn the heat down and bake for 10 minutes more.

In a small saucepan melt the chocolate with the rice milk. Unmold the muffins and dip half of each one in the melted chocolate. Cool in racks.

GRAPEFRUIT FINANCIERS

These lovely bites, flourless and very tender, are also delicious with lemon peel instead of grapefruit essential oil. They are good served with creams, flans, compotes, and tea!

Ingredients for 15 financiers:

- 4 eggs
- 1 cup (100 g) almond flour
- ½ cup (50 g) confectioners' sugar
- 6 drops grapefruit essence

Method:

Separate the eggs. Put the yolks in a bowl and mix with the almond flour. In another bowl beat the whites with confectioners' sugar until firm.

Add the grapefruit essence to the egg yolks-almond mixture. Blend in a tablespoon of egg whites and fold in the rest carefully.

Pour the batter into a rectangular mini baking pan, greased. Bake for 10 to 15 minutes in a medium-heat oven, until golden brown. Unmold while still warm and cool completely before serving.

TEA TIME MADELEINES

These light and fragrant madeleines are delicious with tea for a gourmet breakfast or a comforting snack. If you use raw brown sugar in the recipe, flavor the bites with cinnamon (½ teaspoon) or orange zest.

Ingredients for 30 small madeleines:

- 2 eggs
- 1 ⅔ cups (366 g) raw brown sugar
- ⅔ cup (125 g) vegetable margarine, at room temperature
- 1 ¼ cups (150 g) rice flour
- 1 tablespoon baking powder
- 5 drops grapefruit essence or 5 drops essence of bergamot or ½ teaspoon lemon zest

Method:

Beat sugar with margarine until creamy (bring to room temperature before using). Add the eggs, rice flour, and baking powder. Add grapefruit essence (or bergamot paired with lemon).

Pour in greased muffin pans (⅔ full). Bake at 400 to 425°F, watching carefully while they are baking. When they turn golden brown and grow, they are done. Finally, unmold while warm to prevent the madeleines from sticking to the pans.

AUTUMN BARS

Tender cookies with hazelnut flavor and chestnut perfume. Bake the dough on a baking tray and cut in squares.

Ingredients:

- 1 cup (100 g) chestnut flour
- 1 cup (100 g) almond flour
- ½ cup (110 g) raw brown sugar
- ⅓ cup (50 g) hazelnut paste
- 2 eggs
- 2 tablespoons olive oil
- Vanilla (optional)

Method:

Mix all the ingredients to make a soft dough. Put in a baking tray lined with parchment paper. The dough must be ½ inch thick.

Bake at 375°F for 20 minutes. It is ready when golden brown, but be careful and do not let it overcook.

Take out of the oven, and cut in 1.5-inch squares. Cool completely.

Variation: Add a handful of chocolate chips or chopped hazelnuts to the dough.

10. Crepes

BROWN SUGAR CREPES

These delicate crepes have a mild quinoa perfume. Serve with any fruit compote or marmalade, rice syrup or honey.

Ingredients:

- ⅓ cup + 1 tablespoon (30 g) quinoa flour
- ½ cup (50 g) rice flour
- 2 eggs
- ½-⅔ cup (15-20 cl) soy milk
- 2 ½ tablespoons (30 g) brown sugar

Method:

Combine the flours in a bowl with the rest of the ingredients. Let it rest for 2 hours. If the batter looks too thick, add more soy milk.

Heat a little oil in a skillet and pour in a ladleful of batter. When the first side is cooked, turn the crepe.

RICE FLOUR AND CHESTNUT MILK CREPES

These are light crepes with a delicate fragrance. Serve with citrus jellies, chocolate, chestnut cream, or honey. Chestnut milk is made with an instant powder that dissolves in water.

Ingredients for 6 crepes:

- 2 eggs
- ¾ cup (80 g) rice flour

- 1 tablespoon raw sugar
- ⅔ cup (15 cl) chestnut milk
- 3 drops tangerine essence

Method:

Combine flour and sugar in a bowl. Add the eggs and essential oil. Stir vigorously. Add the chestnut milk. Let it rest for 15-30 minutes. To make light and tender crepes, cook them in a very hot and oiled skillet.

CHESTNUT FLOUR CREPES

These crepes are tender and spongy. Serve with raspberry compote, chestnut cream, or chocolate sauce, also with flambéed apples, honey, chopped hazelnuts, or hazelnut paste.

Ingredients:

- 1 cup + 2 tablespoons (120 g) buckwheat flour
- ⅞ cup (90 g) chestnut flour
- 2 cups soy milk

Method:

Sift the chestnut flour to get rid of lumps. In a bowl combine the flours and soy milk. This helps the batter to maintain a good texture, but you can substitute with rice milk. The batter is slightly thick, therefore it's not necessary to spread the batter too thin to make good crepes. Do not save the batter (after a day or two it ferments and acquires a bitter flavor).

Cook the crepes in a skillet with hot oil. If the first one does not come together, the next one will, because the skillet will then have the right temperature.

11. Creams and Flans

To make dried fruit paste, the fruits must be ground slowly until smooth. Then you can store them in mason jars with or without sugar.

Hazelnut or almond paste goes perfectly with sweet flavors. Besides being rich in nutrients, these ingredients, naturally delicious, are a great addition to desserts and pastries.

Almond paste is soft and can be incorporated in creams, flans, and sweets. Hazelnut has a stronger flavor.

If they are combined with honey or rice syrup, they can be used as fillings for cakes.

On the other hand, if you combine this paste with warm water, they make beautiful vegetable milks.

DISCOVER THE VEGETABLE GELATIN

Agar agar is a natural gelatin extracted from some algae. This ingredient can be found in the form of leaves or flakes, and in powder, ready to be used. This is a healthy gelatin and is very soft (they say it protects the digestive system). Agar agar has a neutral flavor that makes it very easy to use in desserts and other preparations.

RICE PUDDING WITH ORANGE FLOWER WATER

This pudding is made with a vegetable milk (rice or almond) and makes a light dessert. It's a good idea to serve it as dessert in glass yogurt jars or small mason jars. This is a practical idea if you make it in advance and keep it refrigerated.

Ingredients:
- ½ cup (100 g) short grain rice
- 1 ½ cups + 1 tablespoon (35 cl) water
- 4 tablespoons rice syrup
- ⅓ cup (10 cl) rice or almond milk
- 1 tablespoon orange flower water
- fresh pineapple rounds

Method:
Place the rice in a saucepan and add the water. Cook over low heat for 25 minutes or until it absorbs the water. Take off the

heat, and add rice syrup, rice milk, and orange flower water. Mix carefully and let rest.

Pour the pudding in small mason jars (yogurt or marmalade jars will do). Put the lid on and refrigerate. Serve the rice with pineapple.

PINEAPPLE CRÈME BRÛLEE

This dessert is easy and quick to prepare, with an exotic perfume. It is served in small ramekins and is great for festive gatherings.

Ingredients:
- 12 oz (300 g) fresh pineapple
- 3 eggs
- ¼ cup (110 g) raw brown sugar
- ⅓ cup (30 g) rice flour

Method:
Peel the pineapple. Discard the core and place the pulp in the jar of a blender. Add eggs, sugar, and rice flour, and process until smooth. Pour in a baking pan or four ramekins. Bake in a preheated oven at 350°F for 20 minutes.

Serve warm if you want it creamy, or put it in the refrigerator and serve it with heavy cream.

ALMOND AND CHESTNUT CREAM

You can serve this easy recipe with several desserts, such as chocolate tart, for example.

Ingredients:
- 1 cup (100 g) chestnut flour
- 4 cups almond milk (condensed)
- 3 tablespoons honey or maple syrup

Method:
Sift the chestnut flour to avoid lumps. In a saucepan dissolve the flour with almond milk, and cook over low heat, stirring constantly.

Add honey or maple syrup, stirring until dissolved and the cream thickens, for about 5 minutes. Pour in glasses. Cool.

JELLY WITH VERBENA

The thickener here is agar agar mixed with vegetable milk. Verbena water is added at the last minute to add a crisp fragrance. This is sweet, quick, and simple to make. You will have dessert ready in a few minutes.

Ingredients:

- 2 cups rice or almond milk
- 1 teaspoon (2 g) agar agar powder
- 2 tablespoons raw brown sugar
- 2 tablespoons verbena water

Method:

The vegetable milks have a mildly sweet flavor that goes very well with the subtle scent of verbena water.

In a saucepan combine agar agar with the vegetable milk, add sugar, and cook over low heat. When the mixture boils, stir frequently for 2 or 3 minutes.

Turn off the heat, add the verbena water, and pour the mixture in dessert glasses.

Refrigerate until firm.

Serve cold.

CHESTNUT TERRINE WITH CHOCOLATE

This chestnut and chocolate terrine is easy to make, and has a light and creamy texture. Less sugar may be used in our desserts, as the chocolate combined with vegetable milks and chestnut puree will give enough sweetness to the dish. If a sweeter taste is desired, use sweetened vegetable milk with vanilla (or almond-hazelnut) flavor.

Ingredients:
- 1 cup rice milk, soy or almond
- 1 teaspoon (2 g) agar agar powder
- 1 (370 g) jar chestnut puree, unsweetened
- ⅔ cup (100 g) dark chocolate

Method:

Put the chocolate in a saucepan with milk and agar agar. Cook over low heat, stirring continuously for 2 minutes.

Put the chestnut puree in a bowl, add the hot vegetable milk, and stir until smooth. Pour into a loaf pan (you can use a glass or porcelain pan to unmold the dessert) and refrigerate overnight.

RASPBERRY CUP

This is a quick dessert, creamy and sweet. Add half a cup of liquid soy cream to make it smoother. The sweetener used here is agave syrup, which won't hide the natural flavor of the raspberries.

Ingredients:
- 1 ¼ cups (120 g) millet semolina
- 2 cups + 2 tablespoons (50 cl) rice or soy milk
- 5 tablespoons agave syrup (or rice syrup)
- 1 cup raspberry cream (or apricot, rhubarb, or cherry puree)
- ½ cup liquid soy cream (optional)

Method:

Combine the semolina and the vegetable milk. Bring to a boil over low heat, stirring continuously because it will thicken in about a minute.

Add the agave syrup. Put the raspberry cream in dessert glasses and top with the semolina mixture. Refrigerate.

AMARANTH WITH CHOCOLATE

This dessert will surprise your guests' palate, because amaranth is a tiny seed (smaller than quinoa) and rich in nutrients.

Ingredients:

- ½ cup (100 g) amaranth
- 1 ½ cups (30 cl) water
- ⅔ cup (100 g) chocolate
- 2 tablespoons hazelnut paste
- 4 tablespoons rice syrup
- A handful of almonds, coarsely chopped

Method:

Put the amaranth and water in a saucepan and bring to a boil. Cook slowly until the seeds absorb most of the liquid, for about 30 minutes. Cover and cool. In the cooling process, the seeds will turn sticky and this will give the dessert a different texture.

Chop the chocolate and put it in a saucepan over low heat with a few tablespoons of water until it melts. Add the rice syrup and hazelnut paste, stir, and add the cooled amaranth. Turn off the heat. Stir vigorously and add the chopped almonds. Pour in dessert glasses and refrigerate.

CHESTNUT CUSTARD

This silky cream is perfect to serve with cookies or chestnut or chocolate cakes. The orange fragrance marries well with the chestnut. If you don't have orange essence, use orange zest.

Ingredients:

- 4 egg yolks
- ⅞ cup (193 g) raw brown sugar
- ⅔ cup (60 g) chestnut flour

- 4 ½ cups (90 cl) rice milk
- 6 drops orange essence

Method:

In a saucepan mix egg yolks with sugar. Add chestnut flour and the rice milk, little by little. Simmer over low heat, stirring continuously until the cream thickens and lightly covers the spoon. Add the orange essence.

Turn off the heat, pour in dessert glasses, and cool.

FRANGIPANI AND PLUMS WITH ORANGE FLOWER WATER

This frangipani is made with a base of a pastry cream, and goes well with plums macerated in orange flower water. It's best if made in advance or several hours before serving time. Frangipani is great for pies or tarts.

Ingredients:

- 2 egg yolks
- ½ cup (125 g) raw sugar
- ⅓ cup (40 g) rice flour
- 1 ½ cups (30 cl) rice or almond milk
- 3 tablespoons almond paste

To make in advance:

- 12 oz (350 g) plums
- ¾ cup (15 cl) orange flower water

Method:

Place the plums in a bowl, add orange flower water, and add water to cover the plums. Let them macerate.

For the cream, in a small saucepan combine egg yolks and sugar. Add rice flour to the egg mixture, then add the vegetable milk and heat over low heat. Stir vigorously until thick. Turn off the heat, add the almond paste, and cool.

Serve this cream over drained plums. You may drink the orange flower water.

CHOCOLATE FLAN WITH FOUR SPICES

This light flan is made with agar agar. It goes well with madeleines or cookies.

Ingredients:
- 2 cups vanilla-flavored soy milk (unsweetened)
- 2 tablespoons raw brown sugar
- 2 tablespoons ground cacao
- ½ vanilla bean (optional)
- 1 teaspoon (2 g) agar agar powder
- Pinch of cinnamon

Method:

In a saucepan put cacao, sugar, cinnamon, and agar agar. Dissolve everything with soy milk. Slice the vanilla lengthwise and scrap the seeds into the soy milk. Bring to a boil over low heat, and boil for 3 minutes, stirring constantly.

Pour the flan in ramekins or a dessert glass and refrigerate for at least 2 hours before serving.

VANILLA PASTRY CREAM

This is a basic recipe to make many delicious desserts. Its vanilla flavor goes well with everything, but you can give it a rich caramel flavor with licorice, if you substitute raw brown sugar with dark brown sugar.

Ingredients:
- 4 egg yolks
- ⅞ cup (193 g) raw brown sugar
- ¾ cup (80 g) rice flour
- 2 ½ cups (60 cl) rice milk (or soy)
- 1 vanilla bean

Method:

In a small saucepan mix egg yolks with sugar. Add the rice flour to the egg mixture and the vegetable milk.

Slice the vanilla bean lengthwise and scrape the seeds with the tip of a knife. Add them to the mixture and stir. Cook over low heat, stirring continuously until thick.

The cream is ready to enjoy cold, as dessert, to serve with fruit, or as a pie or tart filling.

12. Breakfast

AWAKENING CREAM

Take advantage of the many sprouted seeds to lighten our mornings with this cream, which is very easy to make and will give your palate a sweet start to the day.

Ingredients:

- A handful of sprouted seeds (sunflower or quinoa)
- ¼ cup (60 g) rice cream (precooked flour)
- 1 ⅓ cups (30 cl) almond, hazelnut, rice or soy milk
- 3 or 4 tablespoons agave syrup or rice syrup
- 1 tablespoon almond paste
- A few dry apple cubes
- Raisins (optional)

Method:

Combine rice cream and vegetable milk in a saucepan. Bring to a boil over low heat and cook for 5 minutes or until it thickens. Stir continuously.

Turn off the heat, add the almond paste, and stir well. Sweeten to taste with the agave or rice syrup.

Pour in dessert glasses and sprinkle with sprouted seeds and dry apple cubes.

QUINOA CREAM WITH CHOCOLATE

A delicious cream with chocolate to have for breakfast, so rich in flavor that it could be served as dessert. Substitute sugar for agave syrup, but add it after the cooking because the heat makes it bitter.

Ingredients:

- ⅓ cup (50 g) quinoa cream
- 1 ¾ cups (40 cl) rice milk (or almond milk)
- 2 tablespoons raw brown sugar (or maple or agave syrup)
- 2 tablespoons cacao
- 3 drops orange essential oil

Method:

Combine quinoa cream, sugar, and cacao in a saucepan with the rice milk. Bring to a boil over low heat, stirring continuously until thick. Turn off the heat. Serve in dessert glasses or as a side with cake or tart.

MUESLI WITH QUINOA SEEDS

A sweet tabbouleh-like breakfast; it is very easy to add seasonal fruits or different flavors to this dish.

Ingredients:

- 1 cup quinoa
- 1 ½ cups (30 cl) water
- 2 pears (or any other fresh fruit)
- A handful of raisins
- ⅓ cup (15 cl) quinoa milk
- 3 or 4 tablespoons rice syrup
- 1 teaspoon cinnamon

Method:

Put the quinoa, water, pears, and raisins in a saucepan. Put the lid on and cook over low heat for 15 minutes.

Before serving, add quinoa milk and rice syrup. Dust with cinnamon.

Ideas for the Entire Year

Spring breakfasts

- Mash a very ripe banana and combine with soy yogurt. Use this as cream to spread on gluten-free bread.
- During strawberry season, make a fruit salad and serve with a cream made of cereals, such as rice cream or quinoa cream, lightened with vegetable milk and thickened over low heat. Sweeten lightly with rice syrup (if you want to use a sugar that doesn't spike your blood sugar levels), or a little raw brown sugar. You can use sweetened vegetable milk (almond or rice). These creams are ready in less than 5 minutes and you can make them in advance to have them ready.

Summer breakfasts

- Fruit salads in several colors and flavors: peach, raspberry, or apricot. Take advantage of the summer season to make light rice or quinoa creams, sweets with rice semolina, or little tapioca flans. This is a nice way to familiarize yourself with ingredients that will become your favorites.
- To enjoy the pleasure of toast with summer fruit marmalade, choose apricot, rhubarb, blueberry, raspberry jam, and gooseberry. Spread on cakes or lightly sweetened pastries.

Autumn breakfasts

- Madeleines, cakes, and pastries baked in advance. Delicious creams made with chestnut flour or milk, with the added benefit of hazelnut or almond paste.
- Soak dry fruits the day before (prunes and raisins), which can combine with chopped apples or pears to make a little salad. The almond and chestnut cream, hot or warm, is really good on chilly mornings.

Winter breakfasts

- It is great to prepare in advance to make a crepe batter with chestnut or milk flour. In the morning you will have a quick breakfast and the fillings are really tempting: hazelnut or almond paste, honey, or melted chocolate.
- This is the perfect time of the year to have carrot or pumpkin cake for breakfast, or pudding with chestnut or banana cream. Serve them with apple, pear, or quince compote.

ROMESCO SAUCE (see page 64)

TOMATO AND CORN SOUP (see page 69)

CHINESE SOUP (see page 70)

ZUCCHINI WITH EGGS, HIJIKI, AND OLIVES (see page 71)

QUINOA, CHICORY, AND FENUGREEK SPROUTS (see page 72)

GREEN BEAN SALAD WITH CAULIFLOWER AND POTATO (see page 73)

ASIAN SALAD (see page 74)

BELL PEPPER AND OLIVE QUICHE (see page 76)

COLD CHICKPEA BEAN CROQUETTES WITH SESAME SEEDS (see page 77)

TEMPEH MEDALLIONS GARDEN-STYLE (see page 80)

STEAMED BREAD (see page 86)

CHOCOLATE IMPERIAL (see page 92)

APPLE-CREAM TART (see page 99)

PLUM CRUMBLE WITH CRISPY RICE (see page 108)

DATE COOKIES (see page 114)

TEA TIME MADELEINES (see page 116)

BROWN SUGAR CREPES (see page 118)

CHESTNUT FLOUR CREPES (see page 119)

RICE PUDDING WITH ORANGE FLOWER WATER (see page 120)

CHESTNUT CUSTARD (see page 124)

VANILLA PASTRY CREAM (see page 126)

QUINOA CREAM WITH CHOCOLATE (see page 127)